Python For Beginners : A Step by Step Guide

Anshuman Mishra

Published by Anshuman Mishra, 2025.

ABOUT THE BOOK

PYTHON FOR BEGINNERS: A STEP-BY-STEP GUIDE IS A COMPREHENSIVE INTRODUCTION TO PYTHON PROGRAMMING, DESIGNED SPECIFICALLY FOR THOSE WITH LITTLE TO NO PRIOR CODING EXPERIENCE. WHETHER YOU'RE A STUDENT, A PROFESSIONAL LOOKING TO EXPAND YOUR SKILL SET, OR SOMEONE SIMPLY CURIOUS ABOUT PROGRAMMING, THIS BOOK PROVIDES A STRUCTURED AND EASY-TO-FOLLOW PATH TO MASTERING PYTHON.

PYTHON IS ONE OF THE MOST POPULAR AND BEGINNER-FRIENDLY PROGRAMMING LANGUAGES IN THE WORLD. IT IS USED IN WEB DEVELOPMENT, DATA SCIENCE, AUTOMATION, GAME DEVELOPMENT, AND MORE. THIS BOOK SIMPLIFIES PYTHON'S CORE CONCEPTS, ENSURING THAT YOU UNDERSTAND BOTH THE FUNDAMENTALS AND HOW TO APPLY THEM IN REAL-WORLD SCENARIOS.

EACH CHAPTER BUILDS UPON THE PREVIOUS ONE, OFFERING CLEAR EXPLANATIONS, HANDS-ON EXERCISES, AND PRACTICAL EXAMPLES TO REINFORCE YOUR LEARNING. YOU WILL START WITH THE BASICS—SUCH AS INSTALLING PYTHON AND WRITING YOUR FIRST PROGRAM—AND GRADUALLY PROGRESS TO MORE ADVANCED TOPICS LIKE LOOPS, FUNCTIONS, FILE HANDLING, AND ERROR HANDLING.

BY THE END OF THIS BOOK, YOU WILL HAVE A SOLID UNDERSTANDING OF PYTHON PROGRAMMING AND THE CONFIDENCE TO WRITE YOUR OWN SCRIPTS AND SMALL PROJECTS. THE FINAL CHAPTER INCLUDES MINI-PROJECTS THAT ALLOW YOU TO PUT YOUR KNOWLEDGE INTO PRACTICE, HELPING YOU DEVELOP A PROBLEM-SOLVING MINDSET.

WHY SHOULD YOU READ THIS BOOK? (BENEFITS OF LEARNING FROM THIS GUIDE)

1. BEGINNER-FRIENDLY AND EASY TO UNDERSTAND

THIS BOOK IS WRITTEN IN SIMPLE, CLEAR LANGUAGE, MAKING IT IDEAL FOR ABSOLUTE BEGINNERS. EACH CONCEPT IS EXPLAINED STEP BY STEP, WITH REAL-LIFE EXAMPLES TO HELP YOU GRASP THE LOGIC BEHIND CODING.

2. STEP-BY-STEP LEARNING PATH

THE BOOK FOLLOWS A STRUCTURED APPROACH, ENSURING THAT YOU LEARN EACH TOPIC IN A LOGICAL ORDER. YOU WON'T FEEL OVERWHELMED, AS EACH CHAPTER BUILDS ON WHAT YOU'VE PREVIOUSLY LEARNED.

3. HANDS-ON PRACTICE WITH REAL-WORLD EXAMPLES

LEARNING PROGRAMMING IS MOST EFFECTIVE WHEN YOU APPLY WHAT YOU'VE LEARNED. THIS BOOK INCLUDES PRACTICAL EXAMPLES AND EXERCISES AT THE END OF EACH CHAPTER, ALLOWING YOU TO WRITE AND TEST YOUR OWN PYTHON PROGRAMS.

4. COVERS ALL THE FUNDAMENTAL CONCEPTS

FROM UNDERSTANDING VARIABLES AND DATA TYPES TO MASTERING LOOPS, FUNCTIONS, AND FILE HANDLING, THIS BOOK PROVIDES IN-DEPTH COVERAGE OF THE MOST ESSENTIAL PYTHON PROGRAMMING TOPICS. YOU'LL GAIN A STRONG FOUNDATION THAT PREPARES YOU FOR MORE ADVANCED LEARNING IN AREAS LIKE WEB DEVELOPMENT, DATA SCIENCE, AND AUTOMATION.

5. IMPROVES PROBLEM-SOLVING SKILLS

PROGRAMMING IS ALL ABOUT PROBLEM-SOLVING. THROUGH PRACTICE EXERCISES AND MINI-PROJECTS, THIS BOOK HELPS YOU DEVELOP LOGICAL THINKING AND THE ABILITY TO BREAK DOWN COMPLEX PROBLEMS INTO MANAGEABLE STEPS.

6. CAREER GROWTH AND JOB OPPORTUNITIES

PYTHON IS IN HIGH DEMAND IN VARIOUS FIELDS, INCLUDING SOFTWARE DEVELOPMENT, DATA SCIENCE, MACHINE LEARNING, AND CYBERSECURITY. LEARNING PYTHON CAN OPEN DOORS TO NEW JOB OPPORTUNITIES AND CAREER ADVANCEMENTS. EVEN IF YOU DON'T PLAN TO BECOME A FULL-TIME PROGRAMMER, UNDERSTANDING PYTHON CAN BE A VALUABLE SKILL FOR AUTOMATING TASKS AND WORKING WITH DATA.

7. ENGAGING MINI-PROJECTS FOR PRACTICAL APPLICATION

THE FINAL CHAPTER INCLUDES BEGINNER-FRIENDLY MINI-PROJECTS, SUCH AS:
✓ SIMPLE CALCULATOR – A PROGRAM THAT PERFORMS BASIC ARITHMETIC

OPERATIONS.

✓ **GRADE CHECKER** – A TOOL THAT EVALUATES STUDENT GRADES BASED ON INPUT SCORES.

✓ **NUMBER GUESSING GAME** – A FUN GAME THAT USES LOOPS AND CONDITIONS.

✓ **BASIC STUDENT MANAGEMENT SYSTEM** – A SIMPLE SYSTEM THAT STORES AND RETRIEVES STUDENT RECORDS USING LISTS AND FILE HANDLING.

THESE PROJECTS WILL HELP YOU REINFORCE YOUR LEARNING, BUILD CONFIDENCE, AND MAKE YOUR PYTHON JOURNEY MORE ENGAGING AND ENJOYABLE.

WHO IS THIS BOOK FOR?

- **ABSOLUTE BEGINNERS** – NO PRIOR PROGRAMMING EXPERIENCE IS NEEDED; THIS BOOK IS WRITTEN WITH YOU IN MIND.
- **STUDENTS** – WHETHER YOU'RE STUDYING COMPUTER SCIENCE OR ANOTHER FIELD, LEARNING PYTHON WILL BE A VALUABLE ADDITION TO YOUR SKILLS.
- **PROFESSIONALS** – IF YOU'RE LOOKING TO SWITCH CAREERS OR AUTOMATE TASKS AT WORK, PYTHON CAN MAKE YOUR JOB EASIER.
- **HOBBYISTS & ENTHUSIASTS** – IF YOU HAVE A PASSION FOR LEARNING NEW SKILLS, PYTHON IS A GREAT STARTING POINT FOR EXPLORING PROGRAMMING.

FINAL THOUGHTS

PYTHON IS ONE OF THE EASIEST PROGRAMMING LANGUAGES TO LEARN, BUT MASTERING IT REQUIRES PRACTICE AND THE RIGHT GUIDANCE. **PYTHON FOR BEGINNERS: A STEP-BY-STEP GUIDE** PROVIDES EVERYTHING YOU NEED TO START CODING WITH CONFIDENCE. WITH CLEAR EXPLANATIONS, REAL-WORLD EXAMPLES, AND HANDS-ON EXERCISES, THIS BOOK ENSURES THAT YOU LEARN PYTHON THE RIGHT WAY—BY DOING.

START YOUR PROGRAMMING JOURNEY TODAY AND UNLOCK THE ENDLESS POSSIBILITIES OF PYTHON! 🚀

ABOUT THE AUTHOR

ANSHUMAN MISHRA, AN ACCOMPLISHED ACADEMIC AND EDUCATOR, HAS OVER 18 YEARS OF TEACHING EXPERIENCE AS AN ASSISTANT PROFESSOR IN COMPUTER SCIENCE. HE HOLDS AN M.TECH IN COMPUTER SCIENCE FROM THE PRESTIGIOUS BIRLA INSTITUTE OF TECHNOLOGY, MESRA. CURRENTLY SERVING AT DORANDA COLLEGE, RANCHI, HE SPECIALIZES IN PROGRAMMING LANGUAGES, SOFTWARE DEVELOPMENT, AND COMPUTER SKILLS, INSPIRING COUNTLESS STUDENTS WITH HIS PROFOUND KNOWLEDGE AND PRACTICAL INSIGHTS.

ANSHUMAN IS A PASSIONATE WRITER WITH EXPERTISE IN CREATING EDUCATIONAL RESOURCES FOR STUDENTS AND PROFESSIONALS. HIS BOOKS COVER TOPICS LIKE PYTHON, JAVA PROGRAMMING, SQL, OPERATING SYSTEMS, AND COMPETITIVE PROGRAMMING, REFLECTING HIS DEDICATION TO MAKING COMPLEX SUBJECTS ACCESSIBLE AND ENGAGING.

BEYOND ACADEMICS, ANSHUMAN IS A MOTIVATIONAL THINKER, A LOVER OF MYSTERIES, AND A STORYTELLER AT HEART. HE HAS AUTHORED WORKS RANGING FROM SELF-MOTIVATION GUIDES TO CHILDREN'S STORIES AND BOOKS DELVING INTO THE RICH HISTORY AND CULTURE OF JHARKHAND. HIS ABILITY TO WEAVE KNOWLEDGE WITH INSPIRATION MAKES HIS BOOKS A TREASURE FOR READERS OF ALL AGES.

"Programs must be written for people to read, and only incidentally for machines to execute."
— Harold Abelson & Gerald Jay Sussman, *Structure and Interpretation of Computer Programs*

Copyright Page

Title: **PYTHON FOR BEGINNERS: A STEP-BY-STEP GUIDE**

Author: Anshuman Kumar Mishra
Copyright © 2025 by Anshuman Kumar Mishra

This book is published for educational purposes and is intended to serve as a comprehensive guide for MCA and BCA students, educators, and aspiring programmers. The author has made every effort to ensure accuracy, but neither the author nor the publisher assumes responsibility for errors, omissions, or any consequences arising from the application of information in this book.

TABLE OF CONTENTS

PYTHON FOR BEGINNERS: A STEP-BY-STEP GUIDE

CHAPTER 1: INTRODUCTION TO PYTHON

What is Python?

Python is a high-level, interpreted programming language created by **Guido van Rossum** and first released in **1991**. It has grown to become one of the most popular programming languages globally due to its simplicity, readability, versatility, and wide-ranging application in various fields such as web development, data science, artificial intelligence (AI), machine learning (ML), automation, and more. Python emphasizes readability and simplicity, making it an excellent choice for both beginners and experienced developers.

Overview of Python

1. High-Level Language

Python is considered a **high-level language**, meaning it abstracts away complex machine-level operations. Unlike low-level languages, such as **C** or **Assembly**, which require developers to manage memory allocation, CPU registers, and other hardware-specific details, Python lets developers focus on solving problems without worrying about the underlying machine operations.

- **What does this mean?**: High-level languages, like Python, provide a **user-friendly interface** and hide the intricate details of memory management and hardware-specific instructions. For example, Python handles tasks such as memory allocation automatically, so developers can write more intuitive code without needing to manually manage system resources.
  - **Example**: In Python, you simply declare a variable without specifying memory allocation:

    ```
    x = 10  # Python automatically allocates memory for this
    variable.
    ```

    In contrast, in low-level languages, you would need to manage memory manually using pointers and explicit memory allocation methods.

2. Interpreted Language

Python is an **interpreted language**, meaning the Python interpreter executes the code line-by-line rather than compiling the whole program in advance. This is different from compiled languages, such as **C** or **Java**, where the code needs to be compiled into machine language before running.

- **What does this mean?**: Python code is executed in real-time, which simplifies the debugging process. When an error occurs, Python will stop at the point where the error occurs and provide a detailed error message, allowing developers to fix it immediately.

- o **Example**:

```
a = 5
b = "Hello"
print(a + b)  # This will raise an error
```

- ▪ **Output**:

```
TypeError: unsupported operand type(s) for +: 'int' and 'str'
```

The Python interpreter immediately detects and reports errors, allowing you to fix the problem quickly without recompiling the entire program.

- **Advantages of Interpreted Languages**:
  - o **Immediate Feedback**: Since the interpreter processes the code line by line, you can test each part of the program as you go, rather than waiting for a compilation process.
  - o **Ease of Debugging**: The interpreter halts when an error is encountered and provides detailed error messages, simplifying the debugging process.

3. Dynamic Typing

Python employs **dynamic typing**, which means you do not have to explicitly declare the data type of a variable. The Python interpreter automatically determines the data type based on the value assigned to it.

- **What does this mean?**: You can assign any value to a variable, and Python will figure out the type of that value at runtime. This is in contrast to statically typed languages (such as **C++** or **Java**), where you must declare the type of the variable upfront.
  - o **Example**:

```
x = 10        # x is an integer
x = "Hello"   # Now x is a string
print(x)      # Output: Hello
```

- ▪ In the above example, you did not need to explicitly declare x as an integer or a string. Python automatically adjusts the type of x based on the assigned value.
- **Advantages**:
  - o **Flexibility**: Dynamic typing allows you to change the type of a variable as your program progresses. This can make code faster to write and more flexible.

- **Simplicity**: With dynamic typing, developers don't need to worry about the type of each variable, making the code simpler and easier to understand.
- **Caution**: While dynamic typing enhances flexibility, it can also lead to runtime errors if variables are used inappropriately with incompatible types (e.g., adding an integer to a string).

4. Readable and Clean Syntax

Python is known for its **clean and readable syntax**. The design philosophy behind Python emphasizes code readability, which helps developers understand and maintain code more easily.

- **What does this mean?**: Python's syntax is designed to be simple and intuitive, with minimalistic punctuation and structure. Python code often resembles plain English, making it easy to read, even for people who are new to programming.
  - **Example**:

    ```
    if x > 10:
        print("x is greater than 10")
    else:
        print("x is less than or equal to 10")
    ```

    - In this simple example, the **if-else** condition clearly conveys the logic in a straightforward manner. There are no curly braces ({ }) or semicolons (;) required, as is the case with many other languages like **Java** or **C++**. This reduces unnecessary clutter and improves readability.
- **Why is this important?**:
  - **Maintainability**: Clean and readable code is easier to maintain. As projects grow larger, readable code makes it simpler for other developers to work with your codebase or for you to revisit your code after some time.
  - **Collaboration**: Python's simplicity allows for greater collaboration, as team members can quickly understand each other's code, even if they are not the original authors.

5. Cross-Platform Compatibility

Python is **platform-independent**, which means that Python programs can be run on different operating systems (e.g., **Windows**, **macOS**, **Linux**) without needing any modification to the source code. The Python interpreter takes care of making the program compatible with various platforms.

- **What does this mean?**: If you write Python code on one operating system, it can be executed on other operating systems without any changes. This is because Python abstracts away the differences between operating systems and provides a consistent programming interface across all platforms.

- ○ **Example**: Suppose you write a Python script on a Windows machine that interacts with the file system, and then run that same script on Linux or macOS. The Python interpreter ensures that the code works without any modification, as long as the necessary Python version and libraries are installed.
- **Benefits**:
  - ○ **Portability**: You can develop Python applications on one platform and deploy them on others without needing to rewrite code.
  - ○ **Consistency**: Python ensures consistent behavior across platforms, which is particularly useful in cross-platform applications.
  - ○ **Example**: The following Python code works on all platforms, printing the system's platform name:

```
import platform
print(platform.system())  # Output could be 'Windows',
'Linux', or 'Darwin' (macOS)
```

Key Characteristics of Python

Python is a versatile, high-level programming language widely known for its ease of use and flexibility. Here's a detailed explanation of its key characteristics:

---

1. Easy to Learn and Use

Python is often praised for its straightforward and easy-to-understand syntax, making it an ideal language for beginners, especially those with no prior programming experience. Unlike languages like C++ or Java, which require more complex syntax and strict rules, Python's code resembles natural language, which helps new programmers get started quickly.

Example:

In Python, you don't need to deal with complex syntax to perform simple tasks. For example, adding two numbers can be done with just a few lines of code:

```
a = 5
b = 10
print(a + b)
```

- **Explanation**: Here, two variables a and b are assigned values, and their sum is printed using the print() function. The code is simple and readable. There are no extra semicolons, braces, or complex declarations, which makes it easy for beginners to understand.

Python's design philosophy encourages code readability. The indentation of code blocks (e.g., in loops or functions) is part of its syntax, which enforces a neat and organized structure.

- **Comparison with other languages**: In contrast, languages like C++ or Java require more boilerplate code and complicated syntax. For example, a simple "Hello, World!" in C++ looks like this:

```
#include <iostream>
using namespace std;

int main() {
    cout << "Hello, World!" << endl;
    return 0;
}
```

This is more verbose compared to Python's one-liner:

```
print("Hello, World!")
```

2. Interpreted Language

Python is an interpreted language, which means it executes code line by line. Unlike compiled languages, where the entire program is compiled before execution, Python code is interpreted at runtime, making it easier to test and debug.

Benefits of being interpreted:

- **Immediate feedback**: As you write Python code, it executes immediately, which means you can see results right away. If there's an error, the Python interpreter stops at the problematic line and provides an error message. This makes debugging straightforward because you don't need to recompile the entire program to fix minor errors.
- **Example**: Consider the following Python code with an intentional error:

```
a = 5
b = "hello"
print(a + b)   # This will raise an error
```

- **Output**:

```
TypeError: unsupported operand type(s) for +: 'int' and 'str'
```

- **Explanation**: Python detects that we are trying to add an integer and a string together, which is not supported. The interpreter gives a detailed error message, allowing the programmer to quickly identify and fix the problem.

In contrast, compiled languages like C++ require the entire code to be compiled first. If there is an error, you would need to fix the issue, recompile the program, and then test it again.

3. Dynamic Typing

In Python, you do not need to specify the type of a variable when you declare it. This feature is known as **dynamic typing**. Python automatically assigns the correct type based on the value assigned to the variable.

Example:
```
x = 10          # x is an integer
x = "hello"     # Now x is a string
print(x)
```

- **Output**:

  ```
  hello
  ```

- **Explanation**: Initially, x is an integer (10), and then it's reassigned to a string ("hello"). You don't need to explicitly declare the type of x as int or str. Python handles the type assignment behind the scenes. This flexibility makes Python very easy to use but requires programmers to be cautious about type-related errors, especially when handling data from different sources.
- **Benefit**: Dynamic typing allows for more concise and flexible code. However, it also means that type errors can occur during runtime if you attempt to perform operations that are incompatible with the data types.

4. Platform-Independent

One of Python's major strengths is its **platform independence**. This means that Python programs can run on any operating system (Windows, macOS, Linux, etc.) with little or no modification to the source code. Python achieves this by being an interpreted language, so as long as there is a Python interpreter installed on the system, the same code will execute correctly across different platforms.

Example:

You can write a Python script on a Windows machine and run the same script on a Linux machine without needing to change anything in the code:

```
# A simple Python script that prints system info
import platform
```

```
print(platform.system())   # It will print 'Windows' or 'Linux', etc.
```

- **Output on Windows**:

```
Windows
```

- **Output on Linux**:

```
Linux
```

- **Explanation**: The script works seamlessly across both platforms, demonstrating Python's cross-platform nature. This feature is especially valuable for developers who need to create software that works across multiple operating systems without rewriting code.

---

5. Rich Library Support

Python comes with an extensive standard library and has a huge ecosystem of third-party libraries available. These libraries offer powerful tools and functionalities for virtually every domain, significantly reducing the need to write code from scratch.

Key Libraries:

- **Web Development**:
    - **Flask**: A micro web framework used to build lightweight web applications.
    - **Django**: A full-fledged web framework that simplifies the creation of database-driven websites.
- **Machine Learning**:
    - **TensorFlow**: An open-source machine learning framework for building and training models.
    - **PyTorch**: A popular deep learning library for building neural networks.
- **Data Analysis**:
    - **Pandas**: A data manipulation library for handling structured data, especially useful for working with tables and time series.
    - **NumPy**: A library for numerical computing, offering support for large, multi-dimensional arrays and matrices.
    - **Matplotlib**: A plotting library for creating static, animated, and interactive visualizations in Python.
- **Automation**:
    - **os**: A module for interacting with the operating system, such as working with files and directories.
    - **shutil**: A module for high-level file operations like copying and removing files.
    - **subprocess**: A module for running system commands from Python scripts.

Example:

To demonstrate Python's library support, here is an example of how easy it is to visualize data using **Matplotlib**:

```python
import matplotlib.pyplot as plt

# Data
x = [1, 2, 3, 4, 5]
y = [1, 4, 9, 16, 25]

# Create a plot
plt.plot(x, y)
plt.title('Simple Plot')
plt.xlabel('x')
plt.ylabel('y')
plt.show()
```

- **Output**: A line graph displaying the numbers in the x and y lists.
- **Explanation**: This example shows how Python's powerful libraries make tasks like data visualization simple. By using **Matplotlib**, creating plots becomes an easy task, which would otherwise require complex code in other languages.

Why Python is Popular for Beginners

Python's popularity is not just because of its capabilities but also due to its beginner-friendly characteristics. Here's why Python is widely recommended for newcomers to programming:

1. **Ease of Syntax**:
   - Python has a clean, simple syntax compared to other languages such as C++ or Java. It uses indentation rather than braces { } to define blocks of code, which results in more readable code. For example, printing "Hello, World!" in Python is as simple as:

     ```python
     print("Hello, World!")
     ```

   - In contrast, languages like C++ and Java require more lines of code and more complex syntax to achieve the same result.
2. **Extensive Community Support**:
   - Python has one of the largest and most active communities in the programming world. If you encounter an issue while coding, there's a good chance someone else has faced the same problem. You can easily find solutions or explanations on forums, Stack Overflow, or dedicated Python websites. The large community also contributes to the continuous improvement and evolution of the language.

3. **Wide Range of Applications**:
   - Python is incredibly versatile and can be used in nearly any domain of software development. Some common applications include:
     - **Web Development**: Building dynamic websites and applications using frameworks like Django or Flask.
     - **Data Science**: Analyzing and visualizing large datasets with libraries like Pandas and Matplotlib.
     - **Artificial Intelligence and Machine Learning**: Developing intelligent systems using libraries like TensorFlow, Keras, and PyTorch.
     - **Automation**: Writing scripts to automate repetitive tasks, such as file management, data scraping, and more.
4. **Free and Open Source**:
   - Python is open-source, which means you can freely download, use, and distribute the language. Additionally, most Python libraries are open-source, making them free to use, modify, and share. This has contributed to Python's widespread adoption in both educational and professional environments.

---

2. Applications of Python

1. Web Development

Python is widely used for developing dynamic and scalable web applications. Frameworks like **Django** and **Flask** simplify web development.

Example: A basic Flask app that displays "Welcome to Python Web Development!"

```
from flask import Flask

app = Flask(__name__)

@app.route('/')
def home():
    return "Welcome to Python Web Development!"

if __name__ == "__main__":
    app.run()
```

2. Data Analysis

Python has powerful libraries like **Pandas**, **NumPy**, and **Matplotlib** for analyzing and visualizing data.

Example: Calculate the average of a dataset using Python:

```
import numpy as np

data = [10, 20, 30, 40, 50]
average = np.mean(data)
print("The average is:", average)
```

3. Automation

Python can automate repetitive tasks such as renaming files, sending emails, or scraping websites using libraries like **os** and **BeautifulSoup**.

Example: Rename files in a folder:

```
import os

folder = "my_folder"
for count, filename in enumerate(os.listdir(folder)):
    new_name = f"file_{count + 1}.txt"
    os.rename(os.path.join(folder, filename), os.path.join(folder,
new_name))
```

4. Game Development

Python is used to create 2D games using frameworks like **Pygame**.

Example: A simple game window using Pygame:

```
import pygame

pygame.init()
screen = pygame.display.set_mode((500, 500))
pygame.display.set_caption("My First Game")

running = True
while running:
    for event in pygame.event.get():
        if event.type == pygame.QUIT:
            running = False

pygame.quit()
```

Installing Python: A Detailed Guide

Installing Python on your system is a straightforward process, and the steps vary slightly depending on your operating system (Windows, macOS, or Linux). Below is a detailed guide to help you get Python installed and running on your computer.

Step 1: Download Python

1. Visit the Official Website

- Open a web browser and go to the official Python website: https://www.python.org.

- The website automatically detects your operating system and provides a recommended version for download.
  - o **Windows Users**: Look for a button labeled "Download Python 3.x.x" (e.g., "Download Python 3.10.4").
  - o **macOS Users**: You'll find options for macOS, often labeled as "Download Python 3.x.x for macOS".
  - o **Linux Users**: Python usually comes pre-installed on most Linux distributions, but if you need to install or update it, you can download a specific version from the "All Releases" section.

3. Choose a Version

- **Latest Stable Version**: It is generally recommended to download the latest stable release (e.g., Python 3.x.x) to get the latest features and security updates.
- **Older Versions**: If you need compatibility with older projects or software, you can visit the "All Releases" page to download older versions of Python.

Step 2: Install Python

For Windows:

1. **Run the Installer**
   - o Locate the downloaded file (e.g., `python-3.x.x.exe`) in your Downloads folder.
   - o Double-click the file to launch the installer.
2. **Important: Add Python to PATH**
   - o On the first screen of the installer, **check the box** that says **"Add Python 3.x to PATH"**.
     - ▪ This step is crucial because it allows you to run Python from any command prompt window without additional setup.
3. **Choose the Installation Type**
   - o **Default Installation**: Click the "Install Now" button to go with the standard installation settings, which should be fine for most users.
   - o **Custom Installation**: If you want to change the installation location or customize the features being installed (like enabling `pip`—Python's package manager, or adding `tcl/tk` for GUI support), click "Customize Installation".
     - ▪ Ensure that **pip** and **tcl/tk** are selected if you plan to install third-party libraries or create graphical applications.
4. **Finish Installation**
   - o Click "Install" and wait for the installation to complete.
   - o Once done, you'll see a message saying "Setup was successful". You can now use Python.

For macOS:

1. **Run the Installer**
   - After downloading the `.pkg` file for macOS, double-click it to open the installer.
2. **Follow the Prompts**
   - Click **"Continue"** and follow the instructions to proceed with the installation steps.
3. **Complete Installation**
   - Python will be installed along with **IDLE**, Python's default integrated development environment (IDE).
   - You can now run Python from the terminal or use IDLE for coding.

For Linux:

1. **Check Pre-installed Python**
   - Many Linux distributions come with Python pre-installed. To check if Python is already installed, open a terminal and run:

   ```
   python3 --version
   ```

     - This command should return the installed version (e.g., `Python 3.8.x`). If Python is already installed, you're good to go!
2. **Install Python (if not installed)**
   - If Python is not installed, use the package manager specific to your distribution:
     - **For Ubuntu/Debian-based systems**:

     ```
     sudo apt-get update
     sudo apt-get install python3
     ```

     - This command will download and install Python 3.

Step 3: Verify Installation

1. **Open a Terminal/Command Prompt**
   - **Windows**: Search for "Command Prompt" or "cmd" in the Start menu.
   - **macOS or Linux**: Open the Terminal app from your applications or search for it.
2. **Check Python Version**
   - Type the following command and press Enter:

   ```
   python --version
   ```

     - On macOS and Linux, you may need to use `python3` instead:

     ```
     python3 --version
     ```

- The output should display the installed version of Python, such as:

```
Python 3.10.4
```

3. **Test the Python Shell**
   - To ensure Python is working correctly, you can test the Python shell by typing:

```
python
```

   - On macOS/Linux, use `python3`:

```
python3
```

   - You should see a prompt like:

```
>>>
```

     - This indicates that Python is running and you can start writing Python code interactively.

Step 4: Install an IDE (Optional)

Although Python comes with a basic IDE called **IDLE**, many developers prefer using more advanced tools for a better coding experience. Below are some recommended IDEs and code editors:

1. **IDLE** (Bundled with Python)
   - **Ideal for beginners**, as it's simple, lightweight, and comes pre-installed with Python.
   - It allows you to write and run Python code easily.
2. **Visual Studio Code (VS Code)**
   - **Download**: VS Code
   - **Python Extension**: Install the Python extension for syntax highlighting, debugging, and more advanced features.
   - **Why choose VS Code**: It's a free, feature-rich, and highly customizable code editor that works well for Python development.
3. **PyCharm**
   - **Download**: PyCharm
   - Choose the **free Community Edition** for basic Python development. PyCharm offers powerful features like advanced debugging, project management, and an integrated terminal.
4. **Jupyter Notebook** (Optional)
   - **Ideal for Data Science and Visualization Projects**.
   - To install, open a terminal/command prompt and run:

```
pip install notebook
```

o   Jupyter Notebooks are useful for writing Python code, running it interactively, and documenting it with text, plots, and rich media—great for data science tasks.

Quick Troubleshooting

1. **"Python Command Not Found" Error**
    o   If you encounter an error like **"Python command not found"**, ensure that Python has been added to your system's **PATH** during installation.
    o   **On Windows**, you can manually add Python to the **PATH** by editing the environment variables. Refer to the official Python documentation for detailed steps on modifying the PATH.
2. **Check pip Installation**
    o   **pip** is Python's package manager, and it allows you to install external libraries. To check if pip is installed, run:

    ```
    pip --version
    ```

    o   If pip is missing, reinstall Python and make sure the **"Add pip"** option is selected during installation.

4. Writing Your First Python Program
Introduction to Python IDEs

*   **IDLE:** Python's default IDE; simple and lightweight for beginners.
*   **VS Code:** A powerful, extensible IDE with debugging and plugin support.

Hello, World Program

The "Hello, World!" program is traditionally the first step in learning any programming language.

Example Code:

```
print("Hello, World!")
```

Output:

```
Hello, World!
```

MCQs:

1. **What is Python?** A) A type of snake
   B) A programming language
   C) A text editor
   D) A framework
   Answer: B) A programming language

2. **Which of the following is a key characteristic of Python?** A) It is a compiled language.
   B) It has a simple and readable syntax.
   C) It is a case-sensitive programming language.
   D) It requires manual memory management.
   Answer: B) It has a simple and readable syntax.

3. **Why is Python considered a popular choice for beginners?** A) It is easy to learn and has a straightforward syntax.
   B) It has no libraries or frameworks.
   C) It is a high-level, non-interpreted language.
   D) It is best suited for large-scale applications.
   Answer: A) It is easy to learn and has a straightforward syntax.

4. **Which of the following is an application of Python?** A) Web Development
   B) Data Analysis
   C) Game Development
   D) All of the above
   Answer: D) All of the above

5. **What is the primary purpose of Python in web development?** A) To design graphics for websites
   B) To create interactive webpages and websites
   C) To write system-level programming code
   D) To handle databases
   Answer: B) To create interactive webpages and websites

6. **Python is widely used in data analysis due to its:** A) Speed
   B) Data visualization libraries like Matplotlib
   C) Use in AI and machine learning
   D) Simple syntax for data manipulation
   Answer: D) Simple syntax for data manipulation

7. **What does Python's application in automation primarily involve?** A) Developing operating systems
   B) Automating repetitive tasks like file handling and network tasks
   C) Developing graphics-based user interfaces
   D) Designing computer hardware
   Answer: B) Automating repetitive tasks like file handling and network tasks

8. **Which of the following Python frameworks is commonly used for game development?** A) Django
   B) Flask
   C) Pygame
   D) Pandas
   Answer: C) Pygame

9. **Which of the following is required to install Python on your computer?** A) Downloading a browser
   B) Installing Python from the official website
   C) Setting up a Linux server
   D) Installing only a text editor
   Answer: B) Installing Python from the official website

10. **What is the first step to install Python on Windows?** A) Install a compiler
    B) Download the Python installer from the official website
    C) Install Python through a package manager
    D) Configure environment variables first
    Answer: B) Download the Python installer from the official website

11. **Which IDE is built specifically for Python?** A) Visual Studio Code
    B) Sublime Text

C) IDLE
D) Eclipse
Answer: C) IDLE

12. **What is the purpose of using VS Code as an IDE for Python?** A) It is a text editor with support for multiple programming languages.
B) It only supports Python development.
C) It is slow and difficult to use.
D) It is used only for web development.
Answer: A) It is a text editor with support for multiple programming languages.

13. **What does the following Python program print?**

```
print("Hello, World!")
```

A) Error message
B) Hello, World!
C) World!
D) Hello
Answer: B) Hello, World!

14. **In Python, how do you write a comment in the code?** A) // Comment
B) /* Comment */
C) # Comment
D) -- Comment
Answer: C) # Comment

15. **What is the output of this Python code?**

```
a = 10
b = 5
print(a + b)
```

A) 15
B) 105
C) 50
D) Error
Answer: A) 15

16. **Which Python operator is used for addition?** A) -
    B) *
    C) +
    D) /
    Answer: C) +

17. **What will be the output of the following Python code?**

```
x = 7
y = 3
print(x / y)
```

    A) 2.333
    B) 2
    C) 3.333
    D) 1
    Answer: A) 2.333

18. **What is the result of the expression: `10 % 3` in Python?** A) 3
    B) 10
    C) 1
    D) 0
    Answer: C) 1

19. **Which Python function is used to display output on the screen?** A) print()
    B) input()
    C) output()
    D) display()
    Answer: A) print()

20. **Which Python function is used to get input from the user?** A) input()
    B) read()
    C) get()
    D) print()
    Answer: A) input()

25 questions with answers :

What is Python? Overview and Characteristics

1. **Question:** Briefly define Python and describe three key characteristics that make it stand out.
   - **Answer:** Python is a high-level, interpreted programming language known for its readability. Key characteristics include:
     - Simple syntax, making it easy to learn.
     - Dynamic typing, allowing flexibility in variable usage.
     - Extensive standard library, providing ready-to-use modules.
2. **Question:** Explain the difference between compiled and interpreted languages, and where Python fits in.
   - **Answer:** Compiled languages (like C++) are translated into machine code before execution, while interpreted languages (like Python) are executed line by line. Python is an interpreted language, meaning its code is executed directly by an interpreter.
3. **Question:** What is the significance of Python being "dynamically typed"? Give an example.
   - **Answer:** Dynamically typed means you don't need to declare variable types explicitly. For example, `x = 10` assigns an integer, and later `x = "hello"` assigns a string, without errors.
4. **Question:** Describe the role of the Python interpreter.
   - **Answer:** The Python interpreter reads and executes Python code line by line. It translates the code into machine-readable instructions, enabling the computer to perform the tasks defined in the program.

Why Python is Popular for Beginners

5. **Question:** List three reasons why Python is considered beginner-friendly.
   - **Answer:**
     - Easy-to-read syntax resembling English.
     - Gentle learning curve with clear error messages.
     - Large and supportive community providing ample resources.
6. **Question:** How does Python's readability contribute to its popularity among beginners?
   - **Answer:** Readable code minimizes the cognitive load on beginners, allowing them to focus on understanding programming concepts rather than deciphering complex syntax.

Applications of Python

7. **Question:** Explain how Python is used in web development, and name a popular web framework.

- o **Answer:** Python is used for backend web development, handling server-side logic, database interactions, and API development. Django and Flask are popular web frameworks.
8. **Question:** Describe Python's role in data analysis and name a popular library.
    - o **Answer:** Python is used for data cleaning, manipulation, analysis, and visualization. Pandas is a widely used library for data manipulation.
9. **Question:** How is Python used for automation? Provide an example.
    - o **Answer:** Python automates repetitive tasks like file management, web scraping, and system administration. For example, a Python script can automatically rename and organize files in a directory.
10. **Question:** What are some common libraries used for game development in Python?
    - o **Answer:** Pygame is a popular library for 2D game development.

Installing Python

11. **Question:** Outline the general steps for installing Python on Windows.
    - o **Answer:**
        - Download the latest Python installer from the official website.
        - Run the installer, check "Add Python to PATH," and follow the prompts.
        - Verify the installation by opening the command prompt and typing `python --version`.
12. **Question:** What is the command to verify Python installation on Linux or macOS?
    - o **Answer:** `python3 --version` or `python --version` in the terminal.
13. **Question:** Why is it important to "Add Python to PATH" during installation?
    - o **Answer:** Adding Python to PATH allows you to execute Python commands from any directory in the command line or terminal.

Writing Your First Python Program

14. **Question:** What is an IDE, and why is it useful for Python development?
    - o **Answer:** An IDE (Integrated Development Environment) is a software application that provides comprehensive facilities to computer programmers for software development. It simplifies coding with features like code completion, debugging, and project management.
15. **Question:** Briefly describe the key features of IDLE and VS Code.
    - o **Answer:**
        - IDLE: A lightweight, built-in IDE with a simple editor and shell.
        - VS Code: A powerful, cross-platform IDE with extensive extensions and features for various programming languages, including Python.
16. **Question:** Write the "Hello, World!" program in Python.
    - o **Answer:** `print("Hello, World!")`
17. **Question:** Explain the purpose of the `print()` function in Python.

     ○ **Answer:** The `print()` function displays the specified message or object to the console or standard output.

Practical Examples: Printing Simple Messages

18. **Question:** How do you print multiple strings on the same line using the `print()` function?
    - ○ **Answer:** `print("Hello", "World", end=" ")` or `print("Hello" + " " + "World")`
19. **Question:** How do you print a string on multiple lines using one print function?
    - ○ **Answer:** `print("Line 1\nLine 2\nLine 3")` or `print("""Line 1\nLine 2\nLine 3""")`
20. **Question:** How can you include variables within a printed string?
    - ○ **Answer:** Using f-strings: `name = "Alice"; print(f"Hello, {name}!")`

Practical Examples: Arithmetic Calculations

21. **Question:** Write a Python program to add two numbers and print the result.
    - ○ **Answer:**

    ```
    num1 = 5
    num2 = 10
    sum = num1 + num2
    print(sum)
    ```

22. **Question:** How do you perform integer division and floating-point division in Python?
    - ○ **Answer:**
        - Integer division: `10 // 3` (returns 3)
        - Floating-point division: `10 / 3` (returns 3.333...)
23. **Question:** Write a Python program to calculate the area of a rectangle.
    - ○ **Answer:**

    ```
    length = 5
    width = 10
    area = length * width
    print(area)
    ```

24. **Question:** Explain the order of operations in Python arithmetic calculations.
    - ○ **Answer:** Python follows the standard order of operations (PEMDAS/BODMAS): Parentheses/Brackets, Exponents/Orders, Multiplication and Division (from left to right), Addition and Subtraction (from left to right).
25. **Question:** How do you use the modulo operator (%) in Python, and what is it used for?

- Answer: The modulo operator (%) returns the remainder of a division. It's used to determine if a number is even or odd, or to perform cyclic operations. Example: `10 % 3` returns 1.

practical questions **along with their** answers.

---

1. Write a Python program to check the installed Python version on your system.

Solution:

You can check the installed Python version using the `sys` or `platform` module.

```
# Using sys module
import sys
print("Installed Python Version:", sys.version)

# Using platform module
import platform
print("Python Version:", platform.python_version())
```
Output (Example)
```
Installed Python Version: 3.10.4 (default, Apr 24 2022, 21:03:00)
Python Version: 3.10.4
```

---

2. Write a Python program to display a simple message stating why Python is a beginner-friendly language.

Solution:
```
print("Python is a beginner-friendly programming language because it
has simple syntax, is easy to read, and supports multiple applications
like web development, data analysis, and automation.")
```
Output:
```
Python is a beginner-friendly programming language because it has
simple syntax, is easy to read, and supports multiple applications like
web development, data analysis, and automation.
```

---

3. Write a Python script that automates the task of renaming multiple files in a directory. (Automation Example)

Solution:
```
import os

# Rename all .txt files in the current directory to have a prefix
"new_"
```

```
for filename in os.listdir():
    if filename.endswith(".txt"):
        new_name = "new_" + filename
        os.rename(filename, new_name)
        print(f'Renamed: {filename} -> {new_name}')
```
Explanation:

- This script **automates file renaming** in the current directory by adding "new_" as a prefix to all .txt files.
- It loops through files using os.listdir() and renames them using os.rename().

4. Write a Python program to fetch and display basic statistical data from a dataset using pandas. (Data Analysis Example)

Solution:
```
import pandas as pd

# Creating a simple dataset
data = {'Name': ['Alice', 'Bob', 'Charlie', 'David', 'Emma'],
        'Age': [25, 30, 35, 40, 22],
        'Salary': [50000, 60000, 70000, 80000, 55000]}

# Converting data into a pandas DataFrame
df = pd.DataFrame(data)

# Displaying basic statistical summary
print(df.describe())
```
Output:
```
            Age          Salary
count  5.000000        5.000000
mean   30.400000   63000.000000
std     7.030189   12207.002704
min    22.000000   50000.000000
max    40.000000   80000.000000
```
Explanation:

- This program **simulates data analysis** by creating a dataset and using pandas.DataFrame.describe() to generate basic statistics like mean, count, min, and max values.

5. Write a Python program to install an external library using pip and verify its installation.

Solution:

To install a package (e.g., `numpy`), run the following command in your terminal or command prompt:

```
pip install numpy
```

Then, verify the installation using the following Python script:

```
import numpy
print("NumPy successfully installed! Version:", numpy.__version__)
```

Expected Output:
```
NumPy successfully installed! Version: 1.21.2
```
Explanation:

- The script **checks if NumPy is installed** by importing it and printing its version.

CHAPTER 2: PYTHON BASICS

Variables and Data Types in Python: A Detailed Explanation

In Python, **variables** are used to store data values that can be accessed and manipulated later in the program. Python is a **dynamically typed language**, meaning you don't need to explicitly declare the data type of a variable when you create it. Python will automatically determine the data type based on the value assigned to the variable.

1. Common Data Types in Python

Python supports various **data types** that can be assigned to variables. These include **integers**, **floats**, **strings**, and **booleans**. Let's go over each data type in detail:

1.1. Integers

- **Definition**: Integers represent whole numbers, both positive and negative, without a decimal point.
- **Examples**: `10, -5, 0`
- **Usage**: Integers are used for counting, indexing, and performing arithmetic operations.

1.2. Floats

- **Definition**: Floats (floating-point numbers) represent real numbers and are used for representing numbers with a decimal point.
- **Examples**: `3.14, -2.5, 0.0`
- **Usage**: Floats are used in mathematical calculations that require decimal precision, such as scientific computations or measurements.

1.3. Strings

- **Definition**: Strings are sequences of characters enclosed in either single or double quotes.
- **Examples**: `"Hello", 'Python', "1234"`
- **Usage**: Strings are used to store text, such as names, addresses, or any sequence of characters.

1.4. Booleans

- **Definition**: Booleans represent logical values that can be either **True** or **False**.
- **Examples**: `True, False`
- **Usage**: Booleans are commonly used for making decisions in the code, such as checking conditions in `if` statements or loops.

Code Example: Working with Data Types

Here's a simple example where we define variables with different data types and print their values:

```
# Different Data Types
integer_var = 10        # Integer
float_var = 3.14        # Float
string_var = "Python"   # String
boolean_var = True      # Boolean

# Print the values of variables
print("Integer:", integer_var)
print("Float:", float_var)
print("String:", string_var)
print("Boolean:", boolean_var)
```

Output:

```
Integer: 10
Float: 3.14
String: Python
Boolean: True
```

In this code:

- `integer_var` is assigned the integer value `10`.
- `float_var` is assigned the floating-point value `3.14`.
- `string_var` is assigned the string `"Python"`.
- `boolean_var` is assigned the boolean value `True`.

When printed, the program outputs the values associated with each variable.

---

2. Declaring and Using Variables

In Python, **variables** are created when you assign a value to them using the = operator. Python doesn't require an explicit declaration of the type of variable; it infers the data type from the assigned value.

2.1. Rules for Naming Variables

- A variable name must start with a letter (A-Z, a-z) or an underscore (_).
- The rest of the variable name can contain letters, numbers (0-9), or underscores.
- **Variable names cannot contain spaces or special characters** (e.g., @, #, $, etc.).
- Python is **case-sensitive**, meaning `age` and `Age` are considered two different variables.

2.2. Example of Declaring Variables

```
# Declaring and Using Variables
name = "Alice"  # String
age = 20        # Integer
is_student = True  # Boolean

# Using the variables in a print statement
print(f"My name is {name}, I am {age} years old, and it is {is_student}
that I am a student.")
```

Output:

```
My name is Alice, I am 20 years old, and it is True that I am a
student.
```

- In this example:
  - o name is assigned the string "Alice".
  - o age is assigned the integer 20.
  - o is_student is assigned the boolean True.
- We use **f-strings** (formatted string literals) to combine the variables into a single string and print them in a readable format.

3. Additional Data Types

While integers, floats, strings, and booleans are the most commonly used data types, Python also supports other complex data types like:

3.1. Lists

- A list is an ordered collection of items, which can be of different data types.
- Example: my_list = [1, 3.14, 'apple', True]

3.2. Tuples

- A tuple is similar to a list, but it is immutable (cannot be changed after creation).
- Example: my_tuple = (1, 3.14, 'apple')

3.3. Dictionaries

- A dictionary is a collection of key-value pairs.
- Example: my_dict = {'name': 'Alice', 'age': 20, 'is_student': True}

3.4. Sets

- A set is an unordered collection of unique elements.
- Example: my_set = {1, 2, 3, 3} # Output: {1, 2, 3}`

- **None** is a special data type in Python that represents the absence of a value or a null value.
- Example: `my_var = None`

4. Type Conversion

Python provides several built-in functions for **type conversion**. You can convert one data type to another explicitly, such as from a string to an integer or vice versa.

```
# Type Conversion Example
x = "100"          # String
y = int(x)         # Convert string to integer

print(type(x))   # Output: <class 'str'>
print(type(y))   # Output: <class 'int'>
```

In this example, the string `"100"` is converted to the integer `100` using the `int()` function.

Taking User Input and Displaying Output

1. input() Function

The `input()` function is used to take input from the user. By default, it takes the input as a string.

Code Example:

```
# Taking User Input
name = input("Enter your name: ")
age = int(input("Enter your age: "))

print(f"Hello, {name}! You are {age} years old.")
```

Output: *(Example Input: John, 25)*

```
Enter your name: John
Enter your age: 25
Hello, John! You are 25 years old.
```

The `print()` function displays output. You can format strings using f-strings or `.format()`.

Code Example:

```
# String Formatting
price = 49.99
quantity = 3
print(f"The total cost is: ${price * quantity:.2f}")
```

Output:

```
The total cost is: $149.97
```

Comments in Python

Comments are used to explain the code and are ignored during execution.

- **Single-line Comments**: Start with #.
- **Multi-line Comments**: Enclosed in triple quotes ''' or """.

Code Example:

```
# This is a single-line comment

"""
This is a multi-line comment.
It spans multiple lines.
"""

print("Comments help make code readable!")
```

Basic Arithmetic Operations in Python: A Detailed Explanation

Python supports several basic **arithmetic operations** that are essential for performing mathematical calculations in your programs. These operations include **addition**, **subtraction**, **multiplication**, **division**, **modulus**, and **exponentiation**.

Below, we'll break down each operation in detail and provide examples to help you understand their usage.

1. Addition (+)

- **Definition**: The addition operator + is used to add two values together.
- **Usage**: You can add numbers, strings (concatenation), and other data types that support addition.

Example:
```
a = 10
b = 3

result = a + b
print("Addition:", result)   # Output: 13
```

In this example:

- `a + b` adds 10 and 3, resulting in 13.

2. Subtraction (-)

- **Definition**: The subtraction operator – is used to subtract one value from another.
- **Usage**: This operation can also be used to negate a value (e.g., –a).

Example:
```
a = 10
b = 3

result = a - b
print("Subtraction:", result)   # Output: 7
```

In this example:

- `a - b` subtracts 3 from 10, resulting in 7.

3. Multiplication (*)

- **Definition**: The multiplication operator * is used to multiply two values.
- **Usage**: This operation can be used with integers, floats, and other types that support multiplication.

Example:
```
a = 10
b = 3

result = a * b
print("Multiplication:", result)   # Output: 30
```

In this example:

- `a * b` multiplies 10 and 3, resulting in 30.

4. Division (/)

- **Definition**: The division operator / is used to divide one number by another and returns a **floating-point** result, even if the division is exact.
- **Usage**: Division is performed between two numbers, and the result is always a float.

Example:
```
a = 10
b = 3

result = a / b
print("Division:", result)   # Output: 3.3333333333333335
```

In this example:

- `a / b` divides 10 by 3, resulting in approximately `3.3333333333333335`.

Note: If the result is exact (e.g., `10 / 2`), Python will still return it as a float (i.e., `5.0`).

5. Modulus (%)

- **Definition**: The modulus operator % returns the remainder of a division.
- **Usage**: This operation is useful when you need to know how much is left after dividing two numbers.

Example:
```
a = 10
b = 3

result = a % b
print("Modulus:", result)   # Output: 1
```

In this example:

- `a % b` returns the remainder when 10 is divided by 3, which is 1.

6. Exponentiation ()**

- **Definition**: The exponentiation operator ** is used to raise a number to the power of another number.
- **Usage**: This operation is equivalent to taking the base and raising it to the exponent.

Example:
```
a = 10
b = 3

result = a ** b
print("Exponentiation:", result)  # Output: 1000
```

In this example:

- a ** b raises 10 to the power of 3, resulting in 1000 (since 103=100010^3 = 1000103=1000).

Code Example: All Operations Combined

```
a = 10
b = 3

print("Addition:", a + b)          # Output: 13
print("Subtraction:", a - b)       # Output: 7
print("Multiplication:", a * b)    # Output: 30
print("Division:", a / b)          # Output: 3.3333333333333335
print("Modulus:", a % b)           # Output: 1
print("Exponentiation:", a ** b)   # Output: 1000
```

Output:

```
Addition: 13
Subtraction: 7
Multiplication: 30
Division: 3.3333333333333335
Modulus: 1
Exponentiation: 1000
```

Summary of Arithmetic Operations

Operation	Symbol	Description	Example
Addition	+	Adds two numbers together	10 + 3 = 13
Subtraction	−	Subtracts the second number from the first	10 - 3 = 7

Operation	Symbol	Description	Example
Multiplication	*	Multiplies two numbers	`10 * 3 = 30`
Division	/	Divides the first number by the second, returns float	`10 / 3 = 3.33...`
Modulus	%	Returns the remainder of division	`10 % 3 = 1`
Exponentiation	**	Raises the first number to the power of the second	`10 ** 3 = 1000`

Different Types of Operators in Python

Python supports various types of operators that perform different operations on variables and values. These operators can be categorized into several types based on their functionality. Below is a detailed explanation of each type:

1. Arithmetic Operators

Arithmetic operators are used to perform mathematical operations like addition, subtraction, multiplication, etc.

Operator	Description	Example
+	Addition	`a + b`
-	Subtraction	`a - b`
*	Multiplication	`a * b`
/	Division (returns a float)	`a / b`
//	Floor Division (returns an integer)	`a // b`
%	Modulus (returns the remainder)	`a % b`
**	Exponentiation (power of)	`a ** b`

Example:

```
a = 10
b = 3
print(a + b)   # Addition: 13
print(a - b)   # Subtraction: 7
print(a * b)   # Multiplication: 30
print(a / b)   # Division: 3.333...
print(a // b)  # Floor Division: 3
print(a % b)   # Modulus: 1
```

```
print(a ** b) # Exponentiation: 1000
```

2. Comparison Operators

Comparison operators are used to compare two values and return a boolean result (`True` or `False`).

Operator	Description	Example
==	Equal to	a == b
!=	Not equal to	a != b
>	Greater than	a > b
<	Less than	a < b
>=	Greater than or equal to	a >= b
<=	Less than or equal to	a <= b

Example:

```
a = 10
b = 3
print(a == b)   # Equal to: False
print(a != b)   # Not equal to: True
print(a > b)    # Greater than: True
print(a < b)    # Less than: False
print(a >= b)   # Greater than or equal to: True
print(a <= b)   # Less than or equal to: False
```

3. Logical Operators

Logical operators are used to combine conditional statements and evaluate boolean expressions.

Operator	Description	Example
and	Returns `True` if both operands are `True`	a > 5 and b < 10
or	Returns `True` if at least one operand is `True`	a > 5 or b > 10
not	Reverses the result (True becomes False, and vice versa)	not(a > b)

Example:

```
a = 10
b = 3
print(a > 5 and b < 10)   # True and True => True
print(a > 5 or b > 10)    # True or False => True
print(not(a > b))         # not(True) => False
```

4. Assignment Operators

Assignment operators are used to assign values to variables. These operators combine assignment with other operations.

Operator	Description	Example
=	Assigns the value on the right to the variable on the left	`a = 10`
+=	Adds and assigns the result to the left operand	`a += 5` (equivalent to `a = a + 5`)
-=	Subtracts and assigns the result to the left operand	`a -= 5` (equivalent to `a = a - 5`)
*=	Multiplies and assigns the result to the left operand	`a *= 5` (equivalent to `a = a * 5`)
/=	Divides and assigns the result to the left operand	`a /= 5` (equivalent to `a = a / 5`)
//=	Floor divides and assigns the result to the left operand	`a //= 5` (equivalent to `a = a // 5`)
%=	Takes modulus and assigns the result to the left operand	`a %= 5` (equivalent to `a = a % 5`)
**=	Raises to the power and assigns the result to the left operand	`a **= 5` (equivalent to `a = a ** 5`)

Example:

```
a = 10
a += 5   # a = a + 5 => a = 15
a -= 3   # a = a - 3 => a = 12
a *= 2   # a = a * 2 => a = 24
a /= 4   # a = a / 4 => a = 6.0
```

5. Identity Operators

Identity operators are used to compare the memory locations of two objects.

Operator	Description	Example
is	Returns `True` if both variables point to the same object in memory	`a is b`
is not	Returns `True` if both variables do not point to the same object	`a is not b`

35

Example:

```
a = [1, 2, 3]
b = [1, 2, 3]
c = a
print(a is b)    # False (a and b are different objects in memory)
print(a is c)    # True (a and c refer to the same object)
```

6. Membership Operators

Membership operators are used to test whether a value is a member of a sequence (like a list, tuple, or string).

Operator	Description	Example
in	Returns True if the value is present in the sequence	a in b
not in	Returns True if the value is not present in the sequence	a not in b

Example:

```
a = [1, 2, 3, 4, 5]
print(3 in a)     # True (3 is in the list)
print(6 not in a) # True (6 is not in the list)
```

7. Bitwise Operators

Bitwise operators are used to perform bit-level operations on integers.

Operator	Description	Example
&	Bitwise AND: Returns 1 if both bits are 1	a & b
`	Bitwise OR: Returns 1 if either bit is 1	
^	Bitwise XOR: Returns 1 if bits are different	a ^ b
~	Bitwise NOT: Inverts the bits	~a
<<	Bitwise left shift: Shifts bits to the left	a << 2
>>	Bitwise right shift: Shifts bits to the right	a >> 2

Example:

```
a = 10  # binary: 1010
b = 4   # binary: 0100
print(a & b)  # Bitwise AND: 0 (binary: 0000)
print(a | b)  # Bitwise OR: 14 (binary: 1110)
```

```
print(a ^ b)   # Bitwise XOR: 14 (binary: 1110)
```

8. Ternary (Conditional) Operator

The ternary operator is used for conditional assignment, evaluating a condition and
assigning one of two values based on the result.

Operator	Description	Example
`x if condition else y`	Returns `x` if the condition is `True`, otherwise `y`	`a if a > b else b`

Example:

```
a = 10
b = 5
result = a if a > b else b
print(result)   # 10 (since a > b)
```

Summary Table of Operators

Type	Operator(s)	Description
Arithmetic	`+, -, *, /, //, %, **`	Perform mathematical calculations
Comparison	`==, !=, >, <, >=, <=`	Compare values and return a boolean result
Logical	`and, or, not`	Combine conditional expressions
Assignment	`=, +=, -=, *=, /=, etc.`	Assign and modify values
Identity	`is, is not`	Check if two variables refer to the same object in memory
Membership	`in, not in`	Check if a value is present in a sequence
Bitwise	`&, `	`, ^, ~, <<, >>`
Ternary (Conditional)	`x if condition else y`	Conditional assignment based on a condition

MCQs:

1. **Which of the following is an example of an integer in Python?** A) 10.5
   B) "Hello"
   C) 10
   D) True
   Answer: C) 10

2. **What is the result of the expression** `5 + 3.2` **in Python?** A) 8.2
   B) 8
   C) 3.2
   D) Error
   Answer: A) 8.2

3. **Which of the following is a valid string in Python?** A) "Hello"
   B) 123
   C) True
   D) 3.14
   Answer: A) "Hello"

4. **Which data type does the value** `True` **belong to?** A) String
   B) Integer
   C) Boolean
   D) Float
   Answer: C) Boolean

5. **How do you declare a variable in Python?** A) var x = 10
   B) int x = 10
   C) x = 10
   D) declare x = 10
   Answer: C) x = 10

6. **Which of the following will display** `Hello World` **in Python?** A)
   `print("Hello World")`
   B) `echo("Hello World")`
   C) `write("Hello World")`
   D) `output("Hello World")`
   Answer: A) `print("Hello World")`

7. **What is the correct syntax for taking user input in Python?** A) `input("Enter a value")`
   B) `input[("Enter a value")]`

C) `read("Enter a value")`
D) `get_input("Enter a value")`
Answer: A) `input("Enter a value")`

8. **Which of the following data types can store a decimal value?** A) Integer
   B) Float
   C) String
   D) Boolean
   Answer: B) Float

9. **What will the following code display?**

```
a = 10
b = 5
print(a + b)
```

   A) 105
   B) 5
   C) 15
   D) Error
   Answer: C) 15

10. **What is the output of the following code?**

```
x = "Python"
y = "Programming"
print(x + y)
```

   A) Python Programming
   B) PythonProgramming
   C) ProgrammingPython
   D) Error
   Answer: B) PythonProgramming

11. **Which of the following will correctly format a string in Python?** A)
    `print("Hello {}!".format(name))`
    B) `print("Hello " + name + "!")`
    C) `print(f"Hello {name}!")`
    D) All of the above
    Answer: D) All of the above

12. **Which of the following is the correct way to write a single-line comment in Python?** A) `/* This is a comment */`
B) `# This is a comment`
C) `// This is a comment`
D) `<!-- This is a comment -->`
Answer: B) `# This is a comment`

13. **How can you write a multi-line comment in Python?** A) `/* This is a multi-line comment */`
B) `""" This is a multi-line comment """`
C) `// This is a multi-line comment`
D) `<!-- This is a multi-line comment -->`
Answer: B) `""" This is a multi-line comment """`

14. **What is the result of `10 % 3` in Python?** A) 3
B) 10
C) 1
D) 0
Answer: C) 1

15. **Which operator is used for exponentiation in Python?** A) `*`
B) `/`
C) `**`
D) `^`
Answer: C) `**`

16. **What will be the result of the following Python expression?**

```
3 * 5 + 7 - 2
```

A) 13
B) 18
C) 20
D) 25
Answer: B) 18

17. **Which function is used to output a formatted string in Python?** A) `format()`
B) `print()`
C) `output()`
D) `str()`
Answer: B) `print()`

18. **Which of the following expressions will give the output `True`?** A) `10 == 10`
    B) `10 != 5`
    C) `10 > 5`
    D) All of the above
    Answer: D) All of the above

19. **What will the following code display?**

```
a = 3
b = 4
print(a ** b)
```

    A) 12
    B) 81
    C) 7
    D) 1
    Answer: B) 81

20. **Which of the following will return the remainder of division in Python?**
    A) `//`
        B) `**`
        C) `%`
        D) `=`
        Answer: C) `%`

25 questions and answers covering Variables and Data Types, User Input/Output, Comments, and Basic Arithmetic Operations in Python:

Variables and Data Types

1. **Question:** What are the four basic data types in Python, and provide an example of each? **Answer:** The four basic data types are: * Integers (int): `5` * Floats (float): `3.14` * Strings (str): `"Hello"` * Booleans (bool): `True`

2. **Question:** How do you declare a variable in Python, and what are the rules for naming variables? **Answer:** You declare a variable by assigning a value to it, e.g., `my_variable = 10`. Rules: * Variable names must start with a letter or underscore. * They can contain letters, numbers, and underscores. * They are case-sensitive.

3. **Question:** Explain the difference between an integer and a float in Python. **Answer:** An integer is a whole number without a decimal point, while a float is a number with a decimal point. For example, `5` is an integer, and `5.0` is a float.

4. **Question:** How do you convert a variable from one data type to another in Python? Provide an example. **Answer:** You can use type conversion functions: `int()`, `float()`, `str()`, `bool()`. Example: `x = "123"; y = int(x)`.

5. **Question:** What is a Boolean data type, and where is it commonly used? **Answer:** A Boolean represents either `True` or `False`. It's commonly used in conditional statements and logical operations.

Taking User Input and Displaying Output

6. **Question:** How do you take user input in Python, and what is the data type of the input? **Answer:** You use the `input()` function. The input is always a string, even if the user enters a number.

7. **Question:** Explain how to use the `print()` function to display output, and provide an example of string formatting. **Answer:** `print()` displays output. String formatting: `print(f"The value is {variable}")`. Example: `name = "Alice"; print(f"Hello, {name}!")`.

8. **Question:** How do you convert user input from a string to an integer or float? **Answer:** Use `int()` or `float()`: `age = int(input("Enter your age: "))`.

9. **Question:** What are f-strings in Python, and why are they useful? **Answer:** F-strings are formatted string literals that allow you to embed expressions inside string literals, preceded by an f. They are useful for clear and concise string formatting.

10. **Question:** How do you print multiple variables in a single `print()` statement? **Answer:** Separate variables with commas: `print(var1, var2, var3)`.

Comments in Python

11. **Question:** What are comments in Python, and why are they important? **Answer:** Comments are lines of code ignored by the interpreter. They are important for explaining code and making it more readable.

12. **Question:** How do you write a single-line comment in Python? **Answer:** Use the `#` symbol at the beginning of the line.

13. **Question:** How do you write a multi-line comment in Python? **Answer:** Use triple quotes (`"""` or `'''`) to enclose the comment.

14. **Question:** When should you use comments in your code? **Answer:** Use comments to explain complex logic, provide context, and document code.

15. **Question:** What is the purpose of docstrings in Python? **Answer:** Docstrings document functions, classes, and modules, and are accessed using `help()`.

Basic Arithmetic Operations

16. **Question:** What are the basic arithmetic operators in Python? **Answer:** Addition (+), subtraction (-), multiplication (*), division (/).

17. **Question:** Explain the difference between / and // operators in Python. **Answer:** / performs float division, and // performs integer division (floor division).

18. **Question:** How do you calculate the modulus of two numbers in Python? **Answer:** Use the `%` operator: `result = 10 % 3`.
19. **Question:** How do you perform exponentiation in Python? **Answer:** Use the `**` operator: `result = 2 ** 3`.
20. **Question:** What is the order of operations in Python? **Answer:** Parentheses, Exponents, Multiplication and Division (left to right), Addition and Subtraction (left to right) (PEMDAS/BODMAS).
21. **Question:** How do you perform compound assignment operations in Python? **Answer:** Use operators like `+=`, `-=`, `*=`, `/=`. Example: `x += 5` is equivalent to `x = x + 5`.
22. **Question:** How do you round a float number to the nearest integer? **Answer:** Use the `round()` function: `rounded_num = round(3.7)`.
23. **Question:** How would you get the absolute value of a number? **Answer:** Use the `abs()` function: `absolute_value = abs(-5)`.
24. **Question:** How do you perform integer division and get both the quotient and remainder? **Answer:** Use the `divmod()` function: `quotient, remainder = divmod(10, 3)`.
25. **Question:** How to prevent a division by zero error in python? **Answer:** Use a conditional statement to check if the divisor is zero before performing the division.

```
numerator = 10
denominator = 0

if denominator != 0:
    result = numerator / denominator
    print(result)
else:
    print("Error: Division by zero")
```

25 medium-sized questions and answers:

Variables and Data Types

1. **Question:** Explain the concept of "dynamic typing" in Python and how it relates to variable declaration. **Answer:** Dynamic typing means you don't need to explicitly declare a variable's type. Python infers the type at runtime based on the assigned value.
2. **Question:** What is the difference between a mutable and immutable data type? Which of the basic types are immutable? **Answer:** Mutable types can be changed after creation, while immutable types cannot. Strings, integers, floats, and booleans are immutable.
3. **Question:** How does Python handle type errors when performing operations on variables of different data types? **Answer:** Python raises a `TypeError` when an operation is performed on incompatible types. You need to explicitly convert types using functions like `int()`, `float()`, or `str()`.

4. **Question:** What is the significance of the `None` keyword in Python, and what data type does it represent? **Answer:** `None` represents the absence of a value or a null value. It is its own data type, `NoneType`.
5. **Question:** Describe a scenario where you would use a Boolean variable and how it might affect the flow of a program. **Answer:** Boolean variables are used in conditional statements (e.g., `if`, `while`). For example, `is_valid = True` might determine if a user input is accepted, affecting the program's logic.

Taking User Input and Displaying Output

6. **Question:** How can you ensure that the user input is of a specific data type before proceeding with further operations? **Answer:** Use a `try-except` block to catch `ValueError` if the input cannot be converted to the desired type.
7. **Question:** Explain how to use the `sep` and `end` parameters in the `print()` function. **Answer:** `sep` specifies the separator between printed values, and `end` specifies what to print at the end of the `print()` statement (default is a newline).
8. **Question:** How can you format a float number to display a specific number of decimal places in the output? **Answer:** Use f-strings or the `format()` method: `print(f"{my_float:.2f}")` displays the float with two decimal places.
9. **Question:** Describe a practical example where you would need to combine user input with string formatting to create a dynamic message. **Answer:** Creating a personalized greeting: `name = input("Enter your name: ");` `print(f"Welcome, {name}! We hope you enjoy your visit.")`
10. **Question:** How do you prevent the `input()` function from displaying the input prompt on a new line? **Answer:** The input function always displays the prompt on one line. To prevent the next input from going to a new line, you must change the end parameter of the print statement that might be before the input.

Comments in Python

11. **Question:** Explain the difference between using single-line comments and multi-line comments for code documentation. **Answer:** Single-line comments are for short explanations, while multi-line comments are for longer explanations, docstrings, or temporarily disabling code blocks.
12. **Question:** How can you use comments to document the purpose and parameters of a function? **Answer:** Use docstrings (multi-line comments within triple quotes) at the beginning of the function to describe its purpose and parameters.
13. **Question:** Describe a scenario where you would temporarily comment out a block of code for debugging purposes. **Answer:** When troubleshooting a section of code, you might comment it out to isolate the issue or test alternative implementations.
14. **Question:** How do you ensure that your comments are helpful and maintainable as your code evolves? **Answer:** Keep comments concise, up-to-date, and focused on explaining the "why" rather than the "what."

15. **Question:** How can you use comments to create a to-do list within your code? **Answer:** Use comments like `# TODO: Add feature X` to mark areas that need further attention.

Basic Arithmetic Operations

16. **Question:** Explain how Python handles division by zero and how you can prevent it. **Answer:** Python raises a `ZeroDivisionError`. Prevent it by checking if the divisor is zero before performing the division.
17. **Question:** Describe a scenario where you would use the modulus operator (`%`) and explain its result. **Answer:** Finding if a number is even or odd: `num % 2 == 0` returns `True` if `num` is even.
18. **Question:** How can you use exponentiation to calculate the square root of a number? **Answer:** Raise the number to the power of 0.5: `sqrt = num ** 0.5`.
19. **Question:** Explain how to use the `math` module to perform more advanced mathematical operations. **Answer:** Import the `math` module and use functions like `math.sqrt()`, `math.sin()`, `math.log()`.
20. **Question:** What is the result of performing arithmetic operations on variables of mixed data types (e.g., integer and float)? **Answer:** Python generally promotes the result to the more complex type, usually float.
21. **Question:** How can you use parentheses to control the order of operations in a complex arithmetic expression? **Answer:** Parentheses are used to group operations and override the default order of precedence (PEMDAS/BODMAS).
22. **Question:** How do you round a number to a specific number of significant digits? **Answer:** You can use the round function, along with string formatting, or the decimal module.
23. **Question:** Describe a scenario where you would use integer division (`//`) instead of float division (`/`). **Answer:** When you need the quotient as an integer and don't want any fractional part, such as calculating the number of full pages in a document.
24. **Question:** How do you calculate the power of a number with the built in pow() function? **Answer:** Use the pow() function. pow(base, exponent).
25. **Question:** How to check if a number is a prime number, using basic arithmetic operations, and conditional statements? **Answer:**

```
def is_prime(num):
    if num <= 1:
        return False
    for i in range(2, int(num**0.5) + 1):
        if num % i == 0:
            return False
    return True
```

Practical Examples

1. Simple Interest Calculation

Formula:
$SI=P×R×T100SI = \frac{P \times R \times T}{100}SI=100P×R×T$

Code Example:

```
# Simple Interest Calculation
P = float(input("Enter the principal amount: "))
R = float(input("Enter the rate of interest: "))
T = float(input("Enter the time (in years): "))

SI = (P * R * T) / 100
print(f"The Simple Interest is: {SI}")
```

Output: *(Example Input: P = 1000, R = 5, T = 2)*

```
Enter the principal amount: 1000
Enter the rate of interest: 5
Enter the time (in years): 2
The Simple Interest is: 100.0
```

---

2. Conversion Between Units (Celsius to Fahrenheit)

Formula:
$F=95×C+32F = \frac{9}{5} \times C + 32F=59×C+32$

Code Example:

```
# Celsius to Fahrenheit Conversion
C = float(input("Enter temperature in Celsius: "))
F = (C * 9/5) + 32

print(f"{C}°C is equal to {F}°F.")
```

Output: *(Example Input: C = 25)*

```
Enter temperature in Celsius: 25
25°C is equal to 77.0°F.
```

This section covers essential concepts for beginners and provides practical examples to reinforce understanding. Let me know if you'd like additional examples or explanations!

Example 3: Printing Simple Messages

Python's `print()` function is used to display output.

Code:

```
print("Welcome to Python Programming!")
print("Learning Python is fun!")
```

Output:

```
Welcome to Python Programming!
Learning Python is fun!
```

Example 4: Arithmetic Calculations

Perform simple mathematical operations in Python.

Code:

```
# Arithmetic Operations
a = 10
b = 5

print("Addition:", a + b)
print("Subtraction:", a - b)
print("Multiplication:", a * b)
print("Division:", a / b)
print("Exponentiation:", a ** b)
```

Output:

```
Addition: 15
Subtraction: 5
Multiplication: 50
Division: 2.0
Exponentiation: 100000
```

Example 5: Concatenating Strings

Combine strings using the + operator.

Code:

```
first_name = "John"
last_name = "Doe"
```

```
print("Full Name:", first_name + " " + last_name)
```

Output:

```
Full Name: John Doe
```

Example 6: Using Variables in Messages

Include variables in output messages with f-strings.

Code:

```
name = "Alice"
age = 20

print(f"My name is {name} and I am {age} years old.")
```

Output:

```
My name is Alice and I am 20 years old.
```

Example 7: Area of a Circle

Calculate the area of a circle using the formula πr^2.

Code:

```
# Calculate the area of a circle
radius = 5
pi = 3.14

area = pi * (radius ** 2)
print("The area of the circle is:", area)
```

Output:

```
The area of the circle is: 78.5
```

Example 8: Checking Even or Odd Numbers

Use the modulus operator % to check if a number is even or odd.

Code:

```
number = 7

if number % 2 == 0:
```

```
    print(number, "is even.")
else:
    print(number, "is odd.")
```

Output:

```
7 is odd.
```

Example 9: Swapping Two Variables

Swap the values of two variables without using a temporary variable.

Code:

```
x = 10
y = 20

print("Before swapping:", "x =", x, "y =", y)
x, y = y, x
print("After swapping:", "x =", x, "y =", y)
```

Output:

```
Before swapping: x = 10 y = 20
After swapping: x = 20 y = 10
```

Example 10: Taking User Input

Use the `input()` function to get user input.

Code:

```
name = input("Enter your name: ")
print(f"Hello, {name}! Welcome to Python programming.")
```

Output: *(Example Input: John)*

```
Enter your name: John
Hello, John! Welcome to Python programming.
```

Example 11: Simple Interest Calculation

Calculate simple interest using the formula $SI = \frac{P \times R \times T}{100}$.

Code:

```
# Simple Interest Calculation
principal = 1000  # Principal Amount
rate = 5  # Rate of Interest
time = 2  # Time in years

simple_interest = (principal * rate * time) / 100
print("Simple Interest is:", simple_interest)
```

Output:

```
Simple Interest is: 100.0
```

Example 12: Temperature Conversion

Convert a temperature from Celsius to Fahrenheit using the formula $F = \frac{9}{5} \times C + 32$.

Code:

```
# Celsius to Fahrenheit Conversion
celsius = 25
fahrenheit = (celsius * 9/5) + 32

print(f"{celsius}°C is equal to {fahrenheit}°F.")
```

Output:

```
25°C is equal to 77.0°F.
```

CHAPTER 3: CONTROL STATEMENTS

Control statements in Python manage the flow of execution in a program, allowing decisions to be made or repeating certain actions.

Decision making in Python refers to the process of using conditional statements to determine the flow of execution based on certain conditions. This allows you to execute different blocks of code depending on whether a condition evaluates to True or False.

Here are the three main types of decision-making statements in Python:

---

1. if Statement

The if statement is the simplest form of decision-making in Python. It is used to execute a block of code if a specified condition is True.

Syntax:
```
if condition:
    # Code block to execute if the condition is true
```
Explanation:

- The condition is an expression that evaluates to True or False.
- If the condition evaluates to True, the code block inside the if statement is executed.
- If the condition evaluates to False, the code block inside the if statement is skipped.

Example:
```
x = 10
if x > 5:
    print("x is greater than 5")
```
Output:
```
x is greater than 5
```

- In this example, the condition x > 5 is True because x is 10, which is greater than 5. Hence, the message "x is greater than 5" is printed.

---

2. if-else Statement

The if-else statement provides an alternative block of code to execute when the condition is False. If the condition is True, the code block under the if statement is executed. If the condition is False, the code block under the else statement is executed.

Syntax:
```
if condition:
    # Code block if condition is true
else:
    # Code block if condition is false
```
Explanation:

- The `if` block is executed when the condition is `True`.
- The `else` block is executed when the condition is `False`.

Example:
```
x = -3
if x >= 0:
    print("x is positive")
else:
    print("x is negative")
```
Output:
```
x is negative
```

- Here, the condition `x >= 0` is `False` because `x` is -3. Therefore, the code inside the `else` block is executed, and the message "x is negative" is printed.

---

3. elif Statement

The `elif` statement (short for "else if") is used when you need to check multiple conditions sequentially. It allows you to test several conditions in a sequence and execute the corresponding block of code when a condition evaluates to `True`.

Syntax:
```
if condition1:
    # Code block for condition1
elif condition2:
    # Code block for condition2
else:
    # Code block if all conditions are false
```
Explanation:

- The first `if` block is evaluated. If it is `True`, the corresponding code block is executed, and the rest of the conditions are not evaluated.
- If the first `if` condition is `False`, the `elif` condition is checked, and so on.
- If none of the conditions are `True`, the `else` block is executed (if provided).

Example:
```
x = 0
if x > 0:
    print("x is positive")
elif x == 0:
```

```
    print("x is zero")
else:
    print("x is negative")
```
Output:
```
x is zero
```

- In this example:
  - The condition `x > 0` is `False` because `x` is 0.
  - The `elif` condition `x == 0` is `True`, so the corresponding code block is executed, and the message "x is zero" is printed.
  - The `else` block is not executed because the `elif` condition was met.

Summary of the Three Types of Conditional Statements

Statement	Description	When to Use
if	Executes a block of code if the condition is true	When you need to check a single condition.
if-else	Executes one block of code if the condition is true, and another if it is false	When you have two mutually exclusive choices (one for true, one for false).
elif	Checks multiple conditions in sequence, executing the code block of the first true condition	When you need to check multiple conditions, and one of them should be true.

Example with Multiple Conditions

```
age = 25
if age < 18:
    print("You are a minor.")
elif age >= 18 and age < 60:
    print("You are an adult.")
else:
    print("You are a senior citizen.")
```
Output:
```
sql
Copy code
You are an adult.
```

- In this case, the condition `age < 18` is `False`, so Python moves on to the `elif` statement. Since `age` is 25, which is between 18 and 60, the second condition is `True`, and the message "You are an adult." is printed.

Looping allows you to execute a block of code multiple times. There are two main types of loops in Python: the `for` loop and the `while` loop. These loops allow repetitive execution of code, making it easier to work with a sequence of data or execute a set of actions until a condition is met.

---

1. for Loop with range()

The `for` loop in Python is used to iterate over a sequence (like a list, tuple, string, etc.) or a range of numbers. When iterating over a range of numbers, the `range()` function is commonly used.

Syntax:
```
for variable in range(start, stop, step):
    # Code block
```

- **start:** The value from where the loop starts (inclusive).
- **stop:** The value where the loop ends (exclusive).
- **step:** The value by which the loop counter increases after each iteration (optional, defaults to 1).

Explanation:

The `for` loop assigns each value in the sequence generated by `range()` to the `variable` and executes the code block for each value.

Code Example:
```
# Print numbers from 1 to 5
for i in range(1, 6):
    print(i)
```
Output:
```
Copy code
1
2
3
4
5
```

- **Explanation:**
    - The `range(1, 6)` function generates numbers starting from 1 and ending at 5 (since 6 is exclusive).
    - The loop runs 5 times, printing numbers from 1 to 5.

Customizing the range:

1. **Using a step value:**

```
# Print numbers from 1 to 9 with step 2
for i in range(1, 10, 2):
    print(i)
```

Output:
```
1
3
5
7
9
```

- The `step` value of 2 ensures that the loop increases by 2 with each iteration.

---

2. while Loop

The `while` loop repeatedly executes a block of code as long as the specified condition is `True`. The condition is evaluated before each iteration, and if it evaluates to `False`, the loop is terminated.

Syntax:
```
while condition:
    # Code block
```

- **condition:** The condition is a boolean expression. As long as this condition evaluates to `True`, the loop will continue to execute.

Explanation:

The `while` loop checks the condition at the beginning of each iteration. If the condition is `True`, the code block is executed. If the condition becomes `False`, the loop terminates.

Code Example:
```
# Print numbers from 1 to 5
i = 1
while i <= 5:
    print(i)
    i += 1
```

Output:
```
1
2
3
4
5
```

- **Explanation:**
  - The condition `i <= 5` ensures that the loop continues as long as `i` is less than or equal to 5.
  - After each iteration, `i` is incremented by 1 (`i += 1`), and the loop continues until `i` becomes 6, at which point the condition is `False`, and the loop ends.

Control Statements in Python

Control statements allow you to modify the flow of execution inside loops. The two main control statements used in loops are `break` and `continue`.

1. break Statement

The `break` statement is used to terminate the current loop prematurely. When the `break` statement is encountered, the loop is exited, and the program continues executing the code after the loop.

Code Example:
```
for i in range(1, 10):
    if i == 5:
        break   # Exit the loop when i is 5
    print(i)
```
Output:
```
Copy code
1
2
3
4
```

- **Explanation:**
  - The loop starts iterating from 1 to 9.
  - When `i` becomes 5, the `break` statement is triggered, and the loop exits.
  - As a result, the program prints only numbers 1 to 4 and stops the iteration.

2. continue Statement

The `continue` statement is used to skip the current iteration of the loop and move to the next iteration. When the `continue` statement is encountered, the rest of the code in the current iteration is skipped, and the loop proceeds with the next iteration.

Code Example:
```
for i in range(1, 10):
    if i == 5:
        continue  # Skip the iteration when i is 5
    print(i)
```
Output:
```
1
2
3
4
6
7
8
9
```

- **Explanation:**
    - o The loop iterates through numbers 1 to 9.
    - o When i equals 5, the `continue` statement is executed, which skips the `print(i)` statement for that iteration.
    - o As a result, the number 5 is not printed, but the loop continues with the next numbers (6, 7, 8, and 9).

Summary of Looping Constructs and Control Statements

Concept	Description	Use Cases
for loop	Iterates over a sequence (like a range, list, or tuple)	When you need to iterate over a sequence of data or a range of numbers.
while loop	Continues executing as long as the condition is `True`	When you want to execute code until a specific condition is no longer met.
break statement	Terminates the current loop immediately and exits the loop	To stop the loop when a specific condition is met.
continue statement	Skips the current iteration and proceeds with the next iteration	To skip an iteration and move to the next one, usually for a condition.

3. pass Statement

The `pass` statement is a placeholder and does nothing when executed. It is often used as a placeholder for code that will be added later.

Code Example:

```
for i in range(1, 5):
    if i == 3:
        pass
    else:
        print(i)
```

Output:

```
1
2
4
```

MCQ

1. Which of the following is used to test a condition in Python?
A) `if`
B) `loop`
C) `switch`
D) `return`

Answer: A) `if`

2. What will be the output of the following code?

```
x = 10
if x > 5:
    print("Greater")
else:
    print("Smaller")
```

A) Greater
B) Smaller
C) Error
D) No Output

Answer: A) Greater

3. Which of the following loops is used to iterate over a sequence?
A) `while`
B) `if`
C) `for`
D) `until`

Answer: C) `for`

---

4. Which statement is used to exit a loop prematurely?
A) `continue`
B) `pass`
C) `break`
D) `exit`

Answer: C) `break`

---

5. What will the following code output?

```
for i in range(2, 6):
    print(i)
```

A) 1 2 3 4 5
B) 2 3 4 5
C) 2 3 4 6
D) Error

Answer: B) 2 3 4 5

---

6. What does the `continue` statement do in a loop?
A) It terminates the loop.
B) It skips the current iteration and moves to the next.
C) It stops the program.
D) It does nothing.

Answer: B) It skips the current iteration and moves to the next.

---

7. What will the following code output?

```
x = 5
if x == 5:
    print("Correct")
else:
    print("Wrong")
```

A) Correct
B) Wrong
C) Error
D) No Output

Answer: A) Correct

---

8. Which of the following is used to check multiple conditions in Python?
A) `if-else`
B) `if-elif-else`
C) `switch`
D) `for`

Answer: B) `if-elif-else`

---

9. What will be the output of the following code?

```
num = 10
while num > 0:
    num -= 2
    print(num)
```

A) 10 8 6 4 2 0
B) 8 6 4 2 0
C) 10 6 2
D) Error

Answer: B) 8 6 4 2 0

---

10. Which operator is used to check divisibility in Python?
A) `%`
B) `//`
C) `&`
D) `==`

Answer: A) `%`

---

11. Which loop will run indefinitely if the condition is true?
A) `for`
B) `while`
C) `do-while`
D) All of the above

Answer: B) `while`

12. What does the `pass` statement do in Python?
A) It stops the program.
B) It skips the current iteration in a loop.
C) It is a placeholder for future code.
D) It terminates a function.

Answer: C) It is a placeholder for future code.

13. How do you define a condition in Python?
A) `if (condition)`
B) `if condition`
C) `condition if`
D) `check condition`

Answer: B) `if condition`

14. What will be the output of the following code?

```
num = 12
if num % 3 == 0 and num % 5 == 0:
    print("Divisible by 3 and 5")
else:
    print("Not Divisible by 3 and 5")
```

A) Divisible by 3 and 5
B) Not Divisible by 3 and 5
C) Error
D) No Output

Answer: A) Divisible by 3 and 5

15. Which of the following loops can be used to iterate over a sequence (like a list)?
A) `for`
B) `while`
C) `do-while`
D) None of the above

Answer: A) `for`

---

16. What is the default step size in a `range()` function in Python?
A) 1
B) 2
C) 0
D) -1

Answer: A) 1

---

17. How can we exit a `for` loop in Python?
A) `stop`
B) `exit`
C) `end`
D) `break`

Answer: D) `break`

---

18. What will the following code output?

```
i = 0
while i < 3:
    print(i)
    i += 1
```

A) 1 2 3
B) 0 1 2
C) 0 1 2 3
D) 1 2

Answer: B) 0 1 2

19. What is the correct syntax for an `if-else` statement?
A) `if condition {}`
B) `if condition:`

C) `if (condition): else`
D) `if (condition) else`

Answer: B) `if condition:`

---

20. Which statement is used to skip the current iteration of a loop in Python?
A) `stop`
B) `continue`
C) `break`
D) `exit`

Answer: B) `continue`

25 questions and answers covering Decision Making, Looping Constructs, and Control Statements in Python:

Decision Making

1. **Question:** Explain the purpose of the `if` statement in Python and provide a simple example. **Answer:** The `if` statement executes a block of code if a condition is true. Example: `if x > 0: print("Positive")`.
2. **Question:** What is the `if-else` statement used for, and how does it differ from a standalone `if` statement? **Answer:** `if-else` executes one block if the condition is true and another if it's false, providing an alternative execution path.
3. **Question:** Explain the role of the `elif` statement in Python and how it extends the `if-else` structure. **Answer:** `elif` (else if) allows you to check multiple conditions sequentially, providing more granular control over the program's flow.
4. **Question:** How do you write a nested `if` statement and what are its practical applications? **Answer:** A nested `if` statement is an `if` statement inside another `if` statement. It's used for complex conditional logic, like checking multiple criteria in a hierarchical manner.
5. **Question:** What are logical operators (`and`, `or`, `not`) and how are they used in `if` statements? **Answer:** Logical operators combine or negate conditions. `and` requires both conditions to be true, `or` requires at least one, and `not` negates a condition.

Looping Constructs

6. **Question:** Explain the purpose of the `for` loop in Python and how it iterates through a sequence. **Answer:** The `for` loop iterates over a sequence (like a list or range) and executes a block of code for each item in the sequence.
7. **Question:** How do you use the `range()` function with a `for` loop to iterate a specific number of times? Provide an example. **Answer:** `range(n)` generates a sequence of numbers from 0 to n-1. Example: `for i in range(5): print(i)`.

8. **Question:** What is the `while` loop used for, and how does it differ from a `for` loop? **Answer:** The `while` loop executes a block of code as long as a condition is true. It differs from `for` by not iterating over a predefined sequence.
9. **Question:** How do you create an infinite loop using the `while` loop, and when might this be useful? **Answer:** Set the `while` loop condition to `True`. This is useful for event-driven programs or when you want to loop indefinitely until a specific condition is met.
10. **Question:** How would you iterate through a list using a `for` loop and access both the index and value of each element? **Answer:** Use the `enumerate()` function: `for index, value in enumerate(my_list): print(index, value)`.

Control Statements

11. **Question:** Explain the purpose of the `break` statement and how it affects the execution of a loop. **Answer:** The `break` statement terminates the loop immediately, regardless of the loop's condition.
12. **Question:** What is the `continue` statement used for, and how does it differ from the `break` statement? **Answer:** The `continue` statement skips the rest of the current iteration and moves to the next iteration of the loop.
13. **Question:** Describe a scenario where you would use the `pass` statement and explain its function. **Answer:** The `pass` statement is a placeholder when a statement is syntactically required but no code needs to be executed. It's used for empty blocks or functions.
14. **Question:** How do you use the `break` statement to exit a nested loop? **Answer:** The `break` statement only exits the innermost loop. To exit outer loops, you might need to use flags or restructure your code.
15. **Question:** Describe a practical example of using the `continue` statement to skip specific iterations in a loop. **Answer:** Skipping even numbers: `for i in range(10): if i % 2 == 0: continue; print(i)`.
16. **Question:** What is the else clause in a for loop, and when is it executed? **Answer:** The else clause in a for loop executes when the loop completes normally (without encountering a break statement).
17. **Question:** How do you handle a situation where you need to exit a while loop based on multiple conditions? **Answer:** Use logical operators (`and`, `or`) in the `while` loop condition or include multiple `if` statements with `break` inside the loop.
18. **Question:** What happens if you forget to increment the loop variable in a while loop? **Answer:** You will create an infinite loop.
19. **Question:** How can you use a for loop to iterate through a string and perform an action on each character? **Answer:** Strings are iterable. `for char in my_string: print(char)`.
20. **Question:** Describe a situation where you would use an `elif` ladder instead of multiple independent `if` statements. **Answer:** When you have mutually exclusive conditions and only one block of code should be executed.
21. **Question:** How do you use the `pass` statement to define an empty function that you plan to implement later? **Answer:** `def my_function(): pass`.

22. **Question:** How can you use a `while` loop to repeatedly take user input until a specific keyword is entered? **Answer:**

```
user_input = ""
while user_input != "exit":
    user_input = input("Enter input (or 'exit' to quit): ")
```

23. **Question:** How to use the `break` statement to exit a while loop when a specific condition is met? **Answer:**

```
count = 0
while True:
    if count >= 5:
        break
    print(count)
    count += 1
```

24. **Question:** What is the difference between a for loop with a range and a for loop that iterates through a list directly? **Answer:** A range is used to iterate a certain number of times, while iterating through a list iterates through the elements of the list.
25. **Question:** How do you use nested loops to iterate through a 2D list (a list of lists)? **Answer:**

```
matrix = [[1, 2, 3], [4, 5, 6], [7, 8, 9]]
for row in matrix:
    for element in row:
        print(element, end=" ")
    print()
```

Practical Examples

1. Check if a Number is Positive, Negative, or Zero

Code Example:

```
num = int(input("Enter a number: "))

if num > 0:
    print("The number is positive.")
elif num == 0:
    print("The number is zero.")
else:
    print("The number is negative.")
```

Output:

```
Enter a number: -7
```

The number is negative.

---

2. Print Multiplication Table of a Number

Code Example:

```
num = int(input("Enter a number: "))

print(f"Multiplication Table of {num}:")
for i in range(1, 11):
    print(f"{num} x {i} = {num * i}")
```

Output:

```
Enter a number: 5
Multiplication Table of 5:
5 x 1 = 5
5 x 2 = 10
5 x 3 = 15
5 x 4 = 20
5 x 5 = 25
5 x 6 = 30
5 x 7 = 35
5 x 8 = 40
5 x 9 = 45
5 x 10 = 50
```

---

3. Sum of First N Natural Numbers

Code Example:

```
n = int(input("Enter a number: "))

sum_natural = 0
for i in range(1, n + 1):
    sum_natural += i

print(f"The sum of the first {n} natural numbers is: {sum_natural}")
```

Output:

```
Enter a number: 5
The sum of the first 5 natural numbers is: 15
```

Some Different Practical Examples

1. Check if a Number is Positive, Negative, or Zero

Objective: Use `if-else` statements to check if a number is positive, negative, or zero.

Code:

```python
num = int(input("Enter a number: "))

if num > 0:
    print("The number is positive.")
elif num == 0:
    print("The number is zero.")
else:
    print("The number is negative.")
```

Explanation:
This program prompts the user to input a number and checks if the number is greater than 0, equal to 0, or less than 0. It uses `if-else` and `elif` for decision making.

---

2. Print Multiplication Table of a Number

Objective: Use a `for` loop to print the multiplication table of a given number.

Code:

```python
num = int(input("Enter a number: "))

for i in range(1, 11):
    print(f"{num} x {i} = {num * i}")
```

Explanation:
This program takes a number from the user and prints its multiplication table from 1 to 10 using a `for` loop.

---

3. Sum of First N Natural Numbers

Objective: Use a `for` loop to calculate the sum of the first N natural numbers.

Code:

```python
n = int(input("Enter a number: "))
sum_natural = 0
```

```
for i in range(1, n+1):
    sum_natural += i

print(f"The sum of the first {n} natural numbers is: {sum_natural}")
```

Explanation:
This program calculates the sum of the first N natural numbers by iterating through each number using a `for` loop and adding it to the sum.

---

4. Count Even and Odd Numbers in a List

Objective: Use a `for` loop and `if-else` statements to count even and odd numbers in a list.

Code:

```
numbers = [1, 2, 3, 4, 5, 6, 7, 8, 9, 10]
even_count = 0
odd_count = 0

for num in numbers:
    if num % 2 == 0:
        even_count += 1
    else:
        odd_count += 1

print(f"Even numbers: {even_count}")
print(f"Odd numbers: {odd_count}")
```

Explanation:
This program loops through a list of numbers, checks if each number is even or odd using the modulus operator, and increments the appropriate counter.

---

5. Factorial of a Number

Objective: Calculate the factorial of a number using a `for` loop.

Code:

```
num = int(input("Enter a number: "))
factorial = 1

for i in range(1, num + 1):
    factorial *= i

print(f"The factorial of {num} is: {factorial}")
```

Explanation:
This program calculates the factorial of a number by multiplying all integers from 1 to the given number.

---

6. Prime Number Check

Objective: Check whether a number is prime or not using `if-else` statements and a `for` loop.

Code:

```
num = int(input("Enter a number: "))
is_prime = True

for i in range(2, num):
    if num % i == 0:
        is_prime = False
        break

if is_prime:
    print(f"{num} is a prime number.")
else:
    print(f"{num} is not a prime number.")
```

Explanation:
The program checks if a number is prime by checking divisibility using a `for` loop. If the number is divisible by any number other than 1 and itself, it's not prime.

7. Reverse a Number

Objective: Reverse a given number using a `while` loop.

Code:

```
num = int(input("Enter a number: "))
reversed_num = 0

while num > 0:
    digit = num % 10
    reversed_num = reversed_num * 10 + digit
    num //= 10

print(f"The reversed number is: {reversed_num}")
```

Explanation:
This program reverses a number by extracting each digit using the modulus operator and building the reversed number in the `while` loop.

8. Fibonacci Sequence

Objective: Print the Fibonacci sequence up to the Nth term using a `for` loop.

Code:

```
n = int(input("Enter the number of terms: "))
a, b = 0, 1

for i in range(n):
    print(a, end=" ")
    a, b = b, a + b
```

Explanation:
This program prints the Fibonacci sequence by updating the values of `a` and `b` in each iteration of the `for` loop.

9. Find Maximum Number in a List

Objective: Find the maximum number in a list using a `for` loop.

Code:

```
numbers = [10, 20, 4, 45, 99]
max_num = numbers[0]

for num in numbers:
    if num > max_num:
        max_num = num

print(f"The maximum number is: {max_num}")
```

Explanation:
This program finds the maximum number in a list by comparing each number with the current `max_num`.

10. Check Leap Year

Objective: Check if a given year is a leap year using `if-else` and `elif` statements.

Code:

```
year = int(input("Enter a year: "))
```

```
if (year % 4 == 0 and year % 100 != 0) or (year % 400 == 0):
    print(f"{year} is a leap year.")
else:
    print(f"{year} is not a leap year.")
```

Explanation:
This program checks if a year is a leap year by applying the rules for leap years using `if-else` and `elif`.

---

11. Find Sum of Digits of a Number

Objective: Find the sum of digits of a number using a `while` loop.

Code:

```
num = int(input("Enter a number: "))
sum_digits = 0

while num > 0:
    sum_digits += num % 10
    num //= 10

print(f"The sum of digits is: {sum_digits}")
```

Explanation:
This program calculates the sum of digits of a number by extracting each digit using the modulus operator in a `while` loop.

12. Check Divisibility by 3 and 5

Objective: Check if a number is divisible by both 3 and 5 using `if-else` statements.

Code:

```
num = int(input("Enter a number: "))

if num % 3 == 0 and num % 5 == 0:
    print(f"{num} is divisible by both 3 and 5.")
else:
    print(f"{num} is not divisible by both 3 and 5.")
```

Explanation:
This program checks if a number is divisible by both 3 and 5 using the modulus operator and `if-else` statements.

CHAPTER 4: PYTHON FUNCTIONS

1. What are Functions?

In Python, a function is a block of reusable code designed to perform a specific task. Functions allow you to group a set of statements together to perform a particular action, which makes the code more organized, modular, and easier to maintain. By using functions, we can avoid repeating code, and the program becomes more readable and easier to debug.

Functions are a fundamental concept in Python programming, enabling code reuse, modularization, and efficient organization. When a function is defined, you can call it as many times as needed, providing input (parameters) and receiving output (return values), without rewriting the code.

Purpose of Functions:

1. **Code Reusability:**
   o Functions allow you to reuse a block of code. Once defined, you can call the function whenever needed, avoiding repetition.
2. **Modularization:**
   o Functions break down a complex program into smaller, manageable pieces. Each function performs a specific task, making it easier to understand and work with.
3. **Maintainability:**
   o With functions, you can modify or update a part of the program without affecting other parts. For example, if you change the logic inside a function, you don't need to worry about updating every place the function is used.

Syntax of Functions:

The syntax for defining a function in Python is simple and follows this structure:

```
def function_name(parameters):
    # Code block (the task to be performed)
    return value  # Optional (if you want to return a value)
```

- **def keyword:** Indicates the beginning of a function definition.
- **function_name:** The name of the function, which is used to call it later.
- **parameters (optional):** These are inputs to the function, allowing it to perform operations based on the provided data. Functions can have no parameters, one or more parameters.
- **return statement (optional):** A function can return a value after performing its task. If the function does not return anything, the return statement can be omitted, and it will return None by default.

Breaking it down:

- **Defining a function** with no parameters:

```
def greet():
    print("Hello, world!")
```

- **Calling the function**:

```
greet()  # Output: Hello, world!
```

- **Function with parameters:**

```
def add(a, b):
    return a + b
```

- **Calling the function with arguments:**

```
result = add(10, 5)  # result will be 15
print(result)  # Output: 15
```

Examples of Functions:

1. Function with No Parameters:

A function that doesn't take any input arguments. It simply performs a task and may or may not return a value.

```
def welcome_message():
    print("Welcome to Python Programming!")

# Calling the function
welcome_message()
```

Output:

```
Welcome to Python Programming!
```

- **Explanation:**
    o This function simply prints a welcome message every time it is called.

2. Function with Parameters:

Functions can accept inputs, which can be used in calculations or any other task within the function body.

```
def multiply(x, y):
    return x * y
```

```
result = multiply(4, 5)  # Function call with arguments
print(result)  # Output: 20
```

- **Explanation:**
  - The function `multiply` accepts two parameters, `x` and `y`, and returns their product. When called, it multiplies 4 and 5 and prints the result (20).

3. Function with Return Value:

Functions may return a value after performing some computation or task.

```
def square(num):
    return num ** 2

result = square(7)
print(result)  # Output: 49
```

- **Explanation:**
  - The function `square` takes a number, squares it, and returns the result.

4. Function with Default Parameters:

You can also define functions with default parameter values. This allows the function to be called without providing values for some arguments.

```
def greet(name="Guest"):
    print(f"Hello, {name}!")

greet("Alice")  # Output: Hello, Alice!
greet()         # Output: Hello, Guest!
```

- **Explanation:**
  - The `greet` function has a default parameter `name="Guest"`. If no argument is provided, the default value "Guest" is used. If an argument is provided, it uses the provided name.

---

5. Function with Multiple Parameters:
```
def calculate_area(length, width):
    return length * width

area = calculate_area(5, 3)
print(area)  # Output: 15
```

- **Explanation:**
  - The function `calculate_area` takes two parameters `length` and `width` and returns the area of a rectangle. In this case, it calculates 5 * 3, which is 15.

6. Function with Variable Number of Arguments:

Sometimes, you may not know how many arguments will be passed to the function. Python allows you to handle such cases using `*args` (for non-keyword arguments) and `**kwargs` (for keyword arguments).

Using *args:

```
def add_numbers(*args):
    return sum(args)

result = add_numbers(1, 2, 3, 4)
print(result)   # Output: 10
```

- **Explanation:**
  - The function `add_numbers` accepts any number of arguments (`*args`), and it calculates the sum of all the arguments passed to it.

Using **kwargs:

```
def print_info(**kwargs):
    for key, value in kwargs.items():
        print(f"{key}: {value}")

print_info(name="Alice", age=30)
```

- **Explanation:**
  - The function `print_info` accepts keyword arguments (`**kwargs`), which are passed as a dictionary. The function prints each key-value pair.

Key Points to Remember:

1. **Code Reusability:** Once a function is defined, it can be called multiple times.
2. **Modularization:** Breaking the code into functions makes it more readable and easier to manage.
3. **Parameters and Arguments:** Functions can take inputs (parameters) which allow for more flexibility.
4. **Return Statement:** Functions can return a value. If no return statement is provided, the function returns `None` by default.
5. **Default Arguments:** You can provide default values for parameters, making them optional when calling the function.
6. **Variable Number of Arguments:** Use `*args` and `**kwargs` for functions that take a variable number of positional and keyword arguments.

Functions are essential components of Python, and they can be broadly classified into two categories: **Built-in Functions** and **User-Defined Functions**. Understanding the differences between these two types of functions is crucial for effective programming.

1. Built-in Functions:

Built-in functions are pre-defined functions that are included with Python. These functions perform common tasks that are frequently needed during programming. You do not need to define these functions; they are ready to use out-of-the-box.

Python provides a rich set of built-in functions that make it easy to perform everyday tasks such as data manipulation, mathematical calculations, string operations, and more.

Common Built-in Functions:

1. `len()`:
   - The `len()` function returns the number of items in an object (e.g., a string, list, tuple, dictionary, etc.).
   - It is commonly used to determine the length of collections like strings or lists.

Example:

```
my_string = "Python"
print(len(my_string))   # Output: 6
```

   - **Explanation**: The function returns the number of characters in the string "Python", which is 6.
2. `type()`:
   - The `type()` function returns the type of an object, which can be useful to check the data type of variables.

Example:

```
x = 10
print(type(x))   # Output: <class 'int'>
```

   - **Explanation**: The function returns the type of the variable x, which is an integer (`int`).
3. `round()`:
   - The `round()` function rounds a floating-point number to a specified number of decimal places. If no decimal places are specified, it rounds to the nearest integer.

Example:

```
y = 3.14159
print(round(y, 2))   # Output: 3.14
```

- o **Explanation**: The function rounds the number `3.14159` to two decimal places, giving the result `3.14`.
4. `max()`:
    - o The `max()` function returns the largest item in an iterable or the largest of two or more arguments.

Example:

```
numbers = [1, 3, 2, 8, 5]
print(max(numbers))   # Output: 8
```

- o **Explanation**: The function returns the largest value in the list `[1, 3, 2, 8, 5]`, which is `8`.
5. `min()`:
    - o The `min()` function returns the smallest item in an iterable or the smallest of two or more arguments.

Example:

```
numbers = [10, 20, 5, 15]
print(min(numbers))   # Output: 5
```

- o **Explanation**: The function returns the smallest value in the list `[10, 20, 5, 15]`, which is `5`.

2. User-Defined Functions:

User-defined functions are functions that are created by the programmer to perform a specific task. These functions are not built into Python but are defined by the user using the `def` keyword.

User-defined functions allow programmers to create reusable, modular blocks of code to perform specific tasks, which is one of the most important aspects of writing clean and maintainable code.

Defining a User-Defined Function:

The syntax for defining a user-defined function in Python is as follows:

```
def function_name(parameters):
    # code block
    return value   # optional
```

- **function_name**: The name of the function.
- **parameters**: Optional values that the function can accept. These can be used in the function body.

- **return**: The function can optionally return a value after execution.

Example of a Simple User-Defined Function:
```
def add_numbers(a, b):
    return a + b

result = add_numbers(5, 3)
print(result)   # Output: 8
```

- **Explanation**:
  - The function `add_numbers` takes two parameters `a` and `b`, adds them, and returns the sum.
  - When the function is called with 5 and 3, it returns 8.

Example with Default Parameters:

You can also define user-defined functions with default parameter values.

```
def greet(name="Guest"):
    print(f"Hello, {name}!")

greet("Alice")   # Output: Hello, Alice!
greet()          # Output: Hello, Guest!
```

- **Explanation**:
  - The function `greet` takes an optional parameter `name`, which defaults to "Guest" if no argument is passed.
  - If "Alice" is passed, it prints "Hello, Alice!", and if no argument is passed, it prints "Hello, Guest!".

Key Differences Between Built-in and User-Defined Functions:

Feature	Built-in Functions	User-Defined Functions
Definition	Predefined by Python, no need for user to define them.	Defined by the user for specific tasks.
Availability	Automatically available after importing Python.	Available only after defining them.
Flexibility	Limited to specific tasks.	Highly flexible, can perform any task the programmer defines.
Usage	Typically used for standard tasks like string manipulation, mathematical operations, etc.	Used for custom tasks specific to the needs of the program.

Feature	Built-in Functions	User-Defined Functions
Examples	`len()`, `round()`, `type()`, `max()`, `min()`	Custom functions like `add_numbers()`, `greet()`
Return Values	May or may not return values.	Functions can return values, or can be void (i.e., no return).

Advantages of User-Defined Functions:

1. **Code Reusability**: Functions can be reused multiple times without rewriting the code.
2. **Modular Code**: Breaking down a program into smaller functions makes it more modular and easier to debug.
3. **Maintainability**: By organizing code into functions, it becomes easier to modify or update specific parts of the program without affecting other sections.
4. **Abstraction**: Functions provide a way to abstract complex tasks into simple calls, making the code more understandable.

4. Function Arguments and Return Statements

Function Arguments:

A function can accept arguments (also called parameters) that are used within the function. These arguments are passed inside the parentheses when calling the function.

There are different types of function arguments:

- **Positional Arguments**: These are passed in the order they are defined in the function.
- **Keyword Arguments**: These are passed by explicitly naming the argument in the function call.
- **Default Arguments**: These have a default value if no value is provided during the function call.
- **Variable-Length Arguments**: These are used when a function accepts a variable number of arguments (using `*args` or `**kwargs`).

Example with positional and keyword arguments:

```
def greet(name, age):
    print(f"Hello, {name}. You are {age} years old.")

greet("Alice", 25)  # Positional arguments
greet(age=30, name="Bob")  # Keyword arguments
```

Return Statement:

The `return` statement is used to send a result back from the function to the caller. If no `return` statement is used, the function will return `None` by default.

Example:

```
def multiply(a, b):
    return a * b

result = multiply(3, 4)
print(result)  # Output: 12
```

In this example, the function `multiply()` returns the product of `a` and `b`, and the result is stored in the `result` variable.

5. Practical Examples

Example 1: Write a Function to Find Factorial of a Number

The factorial of a number `n` is the product of all positive integers less than or equal to `n`. The factorial of `n` is denoted as `n!`.

Factorial of a number n:

- `n! = n * (n-1) * (n-2) * ... * 1`
- `0! = 1`

Code:

```
def factorial(n):
    if n == 0 or n == 1:
        return 1
    else:
        return n * factorial(n - 1)

number = int(input("Enter a number: "))
result = factorial(number)
print(f"The factorial of {number} is {result}")
```

Example Output:

```
Enter a number: 5
The factorial of 5 is 120
```

This is a recursive function where the `factorial()` function calls itself until the base case (`n == 0 or 1`) is reached.

Example 2: Check if a String is Palindrome

A palindrome is a word, number, phrase, or other sequence of characters that reads the same forward and backward, ignoring spaces, punctuation, and capitalization.

Code:

```
def is_palindrome(s):
    s = s.lower().replace(" ", "")  # Convert to lowercase and remove
spaces
    return s == s[::-1]  # Check if string is equal to its reverse

word = input("Enter a word: ")
if is_palindrome(word):
    print(f"{word} is a palindrome.")
else:
    print(f"{word} is not a palindrome.")
```

Example Output:

```
Enter a word: madam
madam is a palindrome.
```

In this example, the `is_palindrome()` function first converts the string to lowercase and removes spaces. Then, it compares the string with its reverse (`s[::-1]`) to check if it's a palindrome.

20 Multiple-Choice Questions (MCQs)

1. What is the purpose of using functions in Python?

a) To reuse code
b) To define variables
c) To perform arithmetic operations
d) To display outputs
Answer: a) To reuse code

2. Which of the following is the correct syntax for defining a function in Python?

a) `function my_function():`
b) `def my_function():`
c) `func my_function():`
d) `def: my_function()`
Answer: b) `def my_function():`

3. *What is the keyword used to define a function in Python?*

a) `func`
b) `define`
c) `def`
d) `function`
Answer: c) `def`

---

4. *Which function returns the number of elements in an object?*

a) `count()`
b) `len()`
c) `type()`
d) `sum()`
Answer: b) `len()`

---

5. *What does the `return` statement do in a function?*

a) It prints the output
b) It ends the function
c) It returns a value to the caller
d) It defines the function
Answer: c) It returns a value to the caller

---

6. *What is the output of the following code?*
```
def square(x):
    return x * x

print(square(5))
```

a) `25`
b) `55`
c) `Error`
d) `None`
Answer: a) `25`

---

7. *How can you pass a default value to a parameter in a function?*

a) `def function(a=5):`
b) `def function(a): a=5`

c) `def function(5):`
d) `def function(a, b=5):`
Answer: a) `def function(a=5):`

---

8. *What is the output of the following code?*
```
def greet(name="World"):
    print(f"Hello, {name}")

greet()
```

a) `Hello, World`
b) `Hello, name`
c) `Hello,`
d) `Error`
Answer: a) `Hello, World`

---

9. *Which of the following is a built-in function in Python?*

a) `length()`
b) `max()`
c) `printit()`
d) `divide()`
Answer: b) `max()`

---

10. *What will the following function return?*
```
def cube(n):
    return n**3

print(cube(3))
```

a) 6
b) 9
c) 27
d) 3
Answer: c) 27

---

11. *How can you define a function that accepts an arbitrary number of arguments?*

a) `def function(*args):`
b) `def function(args):`

c) `def function(**args):`
d) `def function(...args):`
Answer: a) `def function(*args):`

---

12. Which of the following is the correct way to call a function?

a) `call function_name()`
b) `function_name()`
c) `invoke function_name()`
d) `function_name.call()`
Answer: b) `function_name()`

---

13. How do you pass multiple arguments to a function?

a) `function(arg1, arg2)`
b) `function(arg1 + arg2)`
c) `function(arg1, arg2, arg3)`
d) Both a and c
Answer: d) Both a and c

---

14. What type of value does a function return if it doesn't contain a return statement?

a) `None`
b) `0`
c) `False`
d) `""` (empty string)
Answer: a) `None`

---

15. What is the default return value of a function in Python if no return statement is given?

a) `0`
b) `None`
c) `False`
d) `""`
Answer: b) `None`

---

16. Which of the following is the correct way to define a function with two parameters?

a) `def function(a, b):`
b) `def function(a+b):`
c) `def function(a, b=5):`
d) `def function(a, b, c):`
Answer: a) `def function(a, b):`

---

17. What is the output of the following code?
```
def check_odd_even(num):
    if num % 2 == 0:
        return "Even"
    else:
        return "Odd"

print(check_odd_even(10))
```

a) `Odd`
b) `Even`
c) `True`
d) `False`
Answer: b) `Even`

---

18. Which of the following is NOT a Python built-in function?

a) `round()`
b) `sorted()`
c) `length()`
d) `type()`
Answer: c) `length()`

---

19. What will be the output of the following code?
```
def add_numbers(a=0, b=0):
    return a + b

print(add_numbers(2, 3))
```

a) `5`
b) `2`
c) `3`
d) `None`
Answer: a) `5`

20. What is the keyword used to define a function in Python?

a) `def`
b) `define`
c) `func`
d) `function`
Answer: a) `def`

25 questions and answers on Functions in Python:

What are Functions?

1. **Question:** Define what a function is in Python and explain its primary purpose. **Answer:** A function is a block of organized, reusable code that performs a specific task. Its purpose is to break down complex tasks into smaller, manageable parts, improve code reusability, and enhance readability.
2. **Question:** Describe the basic syntax for defining a function in Python. **Answer:** The syntax is: `def function_name(parameters):` followed by an indented block of code.
3. **Question:** Explain how to call a function in Python and provide a simple example. **Answer:** Call a function by writing its name followed by parentheses `()`. Example: `my_function()`.
4. **Question:** What is the significance of indentation in defining a function's body? **Answer:** Indentation defines the scope of the function's code block. All indented lines are part of the function.
5. **Question:** Why are functions considered a key component of modular programming? **Answer:** They allow code to be organized into independent, reusable modules, making programs easier to manage and maintain.

Built-in vs. User-Defined Functions

6. **Question:** What is the difference between built-in functions and user-defined functions? **Answer:** Built-in functions are provided by Python (e.g., `len()`, `type()`), while user-defined functions are created by the programmer.
7. **Question:** Provide examples of how to use the built-in functions `len()`, `type()`, and `round()`. **Answer:** * `len("Hello")` returns 5. * `type(10)` returns `<class 'int'>`. * `round(3.14159, 2)` returns 3.14.
8. **Question:** Write a simple user-defined function that adds two numbers and prints the result. **Answer:**

```
def add_numbers(a, b):
    result = a + b
    print(result)
add_numbers(5, 3)
```

9. **Question:** How do you determine if a function is built-in or user-defined? **Answer:** Built-in functions are usually available without importing modules, while user-defined functions are defined within your code or imported from custom modules.

10. **Question:** What are some other common built-in python functions, and what are their purposes? **Answer:** * `print()`: Displays output. * `input()`: Takes user input. * `str()`, `int()`, `float()`: Type conversion. * `max()`, `min()`: Finds maximum and minimum values.

Function Arguments and Return Statements

11. **Question:** Explain the purpose of function arguments and how they are passed to a function. **Answer:** Function arguments are values passed to a function to customize its behavior. They are passed within the parentheses during the function call.

12. **Question:** What is the difference between positional arguments and keyword arguments? **Answer:** Positional arguments are passed in the order defined, while keyword arguments are passed using `name=value` syntax, allowing them to be passed in any order.

13. **Question:** Describe how to use default argument values in a function definition. **Answer:** Assign a default value to a parameter in the function definition: `def my_function(param=default_value):`.

14. **Question:** What is the purpose of the `return` statement in a function? **Answer:** The `return` statement exits the function and returns a value to the caller.

15. **Question:** How do you return multiple values from a function in Python? **Answer:** Return a tuple, list, or dictionary. Example: `return a, b, c`.

16. **Question:** Explain the concept of variable scope in relation to functions. **Answer:** Variable scope determines where a variable is accessible. Local variables are defined within a function and are only accessible inside it. Global variables are accessible throughout the program.

17. **Question:** What happens if a function does not have a `return` statement? **Answer:** It implicitly returns `None`.

18. **Question:** How can you pass a variable number of arguments to a function using `*args`? **Answer:** Use `*args` as a parameter. It collects all positional arguments into a tuple.

19. **Question:** How can you pass a variable number of keyword arguments to a function using `**kwargs`? **Answer:** Use `**kwargs` as a parameter. It collects all keyword arguments into a dictionary.

20. **Question:** Describe a scenario where you would use a function with a return value versus a function that simply prints output. **Answer:** Use a return value when you need to use the function's result in further calculations or operations. Use printing when you just want to display information.

21. **Question:** How can you write a function that modifies a global variable? **Answer:** Use the `global` keyword inside the function: `global my_variable`.

22. **Question:** What are lambda functions in python, and when are they used? **Answer:** Lambda functions are small, anonymous functions defined with the

lambda keyword. They are used for simple operations where a full function definition is not needed.

23. **Question:** How do you pass a function as an argument to another function? **Answer:** Function names can be passed as arguments, treating them as variables.

24. **Question:** How to write a recursive function, and what are the important parts of a recursive function. **Answer:** A recursive function calls itself. Important parts: a base case (to stop recursion) and a recursive call.

25. **Question:** What are docstrings, and how do you use them to document functions? **Answer:** Docstrings are multi-line strings used to document functions. They are enclosed in triple quotes and placed immediately after the function definition. They can be accessed by using the help() function.

Example 1: Simple Function to Add Two Numbers

This function takes two parameters, adds them, and returns the sum.

```
def add_numbers(a, b):
    return a + b

result = add_numbers(5, 7)
print(f"Sum: {result}")
```

Output:

```
Sum: 12
```

Example 2: Function to Calculate the Factorial of a Number

The factorial function calculates the factorial of a given number using recursion.

```
def factorial(n):
    if n == 0 or n == 1:
        return 1
    else:
        return n * factorial(n - 1)

number = 5
result = factorial(number)
print(f"Factorial of {number}: {result}")
```

Output:

```
Factorial of 5: 120
```

Example 3: Checking if a String is a Palindrome

This function checks if a string is a palindrome (reads the same forwards and backwards).

```
def is_palindrome(s):
    return s == s[::-1]

word = "madam"
if is_palindrome(word):
    print(f"{word} is a palindrome.")
else:
    print(f"{word} is not a palindrome.")
```

Output:

```
madam is a palindrome.
```

Example 4: Function to Find the Maximum of Three Numbers

This function compares three numbers and returns the maximum.

```
def max_of_three(a, b, c):
    return max(a, b, c)

result = max_of_three(3, 7, 5)
print(f"Maximum of three numbers: {result}")
```

Output:

```
Maximum of three numbers: 7
```

Example 5: Function to Calculate the Area of a Circle

This function calculates the area of a circle given its radius.

```
import math

def area_of_circle(radius):
    return math.pi * (radius ** 2)

radius = 4
area = area_of_circle(radius)
print(f"Area of circle with radius {radius}: {area}")
```

Output:

```
Area of circle with radius 4: 50.26548245743669
```

Example 6: Function to Count the Occurrences of a Character in a String

This function counts how many times a specific character appears in a string.

```
def count_char(string, char):
    return string.count(char)

text = "hello world"
character = 'o'
count = count_char(text, character)
print(f"Occurrences of '{character}' in '{text}': {count}")
```

Output:

```
Occurrences of 'o' in 'hello world': 2
```

Example 7: Function to Convert Celsius to Fahrenheit

This function converts a temperature from Celsius to Fahrenheit.

```
def celsius_to_fahrenheit(celsius):
    return (celsius * 9/5) + 32

temp_celsius = 30
temp_fahrenheit = celsius_to_fahrenheit(temp_celsius)
print(f"{temp_celsius}°C is {temp_fahrenheit}°F")
```

Output:

```
30°C is 86.0°F
```

Example 8: Function to Check if a Number is Even or Odd

This function checks whether a number is even or odd.

```
def check_even_odd(number):
    return "Even" if number % 2 == 0 else "Odd"

num = 15
result = check_even_odd(num)
print(f"{num} is {result}")
```

Output:

```
15 is Odd
```

Example 9: Function to Reverse a String

This function takes a string and returns its reverse.

```
```

```
def reverse_string(s):
    return s[::-1]

word = "python"
reversed_word = reverse_string(word)
print(f"Reversed string of '{word}': {reversed_word}")
```

Output:

```
Reversed string of 'python': nohtyp
```

Example 10: Function to Find the Sum of Digits of a Number

This function calculates the sum of digits of a given number.

```
def sum_of_digits(number):
    return sum(int(digit) for digit in str(number))

num = 12345
result = sum_of_digits(num)
print(f"Sum of digits of {num}: {result}")
```

Output:

```
Sum of digits of 12345: 15
```

CHAPTER 5: WORKING WITH STRINGS

Strings are one of the most commonly used data types in Python. A string is a sequence of characters enclosed in either single (') or double (") quotes. Python provides a wide variety of methods and operations that allow you to manipulate strings easily.

---

1. Introduction to Strings

Creating and Accessing Strings

In Python, strings can be created simply by enclosing characters in either single or double quotes. To access specific characters in a string, we use indexing.

- **Indexing:** Python allows accessing each character of a string using an index, starting from 0 for the first character.
- **Negative Indexing:** Python also allows indexing from the end of the string, with -1 representing the last character.

Example:
```
# Creating a string
str1 = "Hello, World!"

# Accessing characters
print(str1[0])   # First character
print(str1[-1])  # Last character
```

Output:

```
H
!
```

String Operations: Concatenation, Repetition, Slicing

- **Concatenation:** Combining two or more strings using the + operator.
- **Repetition:** Repeating a string multiple times using the * operator.
- **Slicing:** Extracting a substring from a string by specifying a start index and an end index.

Examples:
```
# Concatenation
str1 = "Hello"
str2 = "World"
result = str1 + " " + str2
print(result)   # Output: "Hello World"

# Repetition
str3 = "Python"
result = str3 * 3
print(result)   # Output: "PythonPythonPython"
```

```
# Slicing
str4 = "Hello, World!"
substring = str4[0:5]
print(substring)  # Output: "Hello"
```

Output:

```
Hello World
PythonPythonPython
Hello
```

2. String Methods

Python provides a number of built-in string methods that can be used for common tasks.

upper() and lower()

- `upper()` converts all characters in the string to uppercase.
- `lower()` converts all characters in the string to lowercase.

```
Example:
str1 = "Hello, World!"
print(str1.upper())  # Output: "HELLO, WORLD!"
print(str1.lower())  # Output: "hello, world!"
```

Output:

```
hello, world!
```
strip()

The `strip()` method removes any leading or trailing whitespace characters (spaces, tabs, etc.) from the string.

```
Example:
str2 = "   Hello, Python!   "
print(str2.strip())  # Output: "Hello, Python!"
```

Output:

```
Hello, Python!
```
split()

The `split()` method divides the string into a list based on a specified delimiter. By default, it splits by whitespace.

Example:
```
str3 = "Hello World Python"
words = str3.split()  # Splits at spaces by default
print(words)  # Output: ['Hello', 'World', 'Python']
```

Output:

```
 ['Hello', 'World', 'Python']
```
replace()

The `replace()` method is used to replace a specified substring with another substring in a string.

Example:
```
str4 = "Hello, World!"
new_str = str4.replace("World", "Python")
print(new_str)  # Output: "Hello, Python!"
```

Output:

```
Copy code
Hello, Python!
```

---

3. Using Strings in Practical Problems

Reversing a String

You can reverse a string using slicing or by using Python's built-in `reversed()` function. Here's how you can do it with slicing:

Example:
```
def reverse_string(s):
    return s[::-1]

str1 = "Hello"
reversed_str = reverse_string(str1)
print(reversed_str)  # Output: "olleH"
```

Output:

Alternatively, you can use the `reversed()` function:

```
def reverse_string(s):
    return ''.join(reversed(s))

str1 = "Python"
reversed_str = reverse_string(str1)
print(reversed_str)  # Output: "nohtyP"
```

Output:

```
nohtyP
```
Counting Vowels in a String

To count vowels in a string, you can loop through the string and check if each character is a vowel.

Example:
```python
def count_vowels(s):
    vowels = "aeiouAEIOU"
    count = 0
    for char in s:
        if char in vowels:
            count += 1
    return count

str1 = "Hello, World!"
vowel_count = count_vowels(str1)
print(f"Number of vowels: {vowel_count}")
```

Output:

```
Number of vowels: 3
```

Summary of Common String Operations

Operation	Description	Example
Concatenation	Join two or more strings together.	`str1 + str2`
Repetition	Repeat the string multiple times.	`str1 * 3`
Slicing	Extract a portion of a string.	`str1[0:5]`
upper()	Convert all characters to uppercase.	`str1.upper()`
lower()	Convert all characters to lowercase.	`str1.lower()`
strip()	Remove leading and trailing whitespace.	`str1.strip()`
split()	Split a string into a list of substrings based on a delimiter.	`str1.split()`
replace()	Replace occurrences of a substring with another substring.	`str1.replace("Hello", "Hi")`

Operation	Description	Example
reverse()	Reverse the string (using slicing or `reversed()` function).	`str1[::-1]`
count()	Count occurrences of a substring in the string.	`str1.count("o")`

MCQs on Strings:

1. What is the output of the following code?
```
str1 = "Python"
print(str1[0])
```

A) P
B) p
C) Error
D) None
Answer: A) P

2. Which method is used to convert a string to lowercase?

A) upper()
B) lower()
C) capitalize()
D) strip()
Answer: B) lower()

3. What is the result of the following code?
```
str1 = "Python"
str2 = "Programming"
print(str1 + str2)
```

A) Python Programming
B) PythonProgramming
C) Error
D) None
Answer: B) PythonProgramming

4. Which method removes spaces from both ends of a string?

A) strip()
B) split()
C) join()
D) replace()
Answer: A) strip()

5. What does the `split()` method return?

A) String
B) List of strings
C) Tuple
D) Dictionary
Answer: B) List of strings

6. What is the output of the following code?
```
str1 = "Python Programming"
print(str1[7:17])
```

A) Python
B) Program
C) Programming
D) Error
Answer: C) Programming

7. What does the `replace()` method do?

A) Replace a substring with another substring
B) Remove all spaces
C) Split the string into a list
D) Change the case of characters
Answer: A) Replace a substring with another substring

8. Which of the following methods converts a string to uppercase?

A) capitalize()
B) upper()
C) lower()
D) title()
Answer: B) upper()

9. How do you reverse a string in Python?

A) `string.reverse()`
B) `reversed(string)`
C) `string[::-1]`
D) `string.reverse()`
Answer: C) `string[::-1]`

10. How do you check if a substring exists in a string?

A) substring in string
B) string.find(substring)

C) string.includes(substring)
D) string.has(substring)
Answer: A) substring in string

11. *Which of the following is the correct way to combine two strings in Python?*

A) string1.combine(string2)
B) string1 + string2
C) combine(string1, string2)
D) append(string1, string2)
Answer: B) string1 + string2

12. *Which method would you use to remove spaces from the beginning and end of a string?*

A) trim()
B) remove()
C) strip()
D) delete()
Answer: C) strip()

13. *What is the result of this code?*
```
str1 = "Hello, World!"
print(str1[7:])
```

A) World!
B) Hello
C) Error
D) None
Answer: A) World!

14. *Which method will help to count the occurrence of a substring in a string?*

A) count()
B) find()
C) search()
D) locate()
Answer: A) count()

15. *What will be the output of the following code?*
```
str1 = "I love Python"
str2 = "Python"
print(str1.find(str2))
```

A) 0
B) 1
C) 7

D) -1
Answer: C) 7

16. What does the `join()` *method do in Python?*

A) Joins elements of a string into a list
B) Joins multiple strings into a single string
C) Joins list elements into a string
D) None of the above
Answer: B) Joins multiple strings into a single string

17. What is the result of the following code?
```
str1 = "Python is fun!"
print(len(str1))
```

A) 10
B) 15
C) 14
D) 13
Answer: C) 14

18. How do you remove a specific character in a string?

A) `str1.delete("o")`
B) `str1.remove("o")`
C) `str1.replace("o", "")`
D) `str1.strip("o")`
Answer: C) `str1.replace("o", "")`

19. Which of the following is a valid Python string?

A) "Hello World
B) Hello World"
C) 'Hello World'
D) Hello World
Answer: C) 'Hello World'

20. Which method returns the character at a given position in the string?

A) charAt()
B) index()
C) str[]
D) None of the above
Answer: C) str[]

questions and answers covering Introduction to Strings and String Methods in Python:

Introduction to Strings

1. **Question:** How do you create a string in Python, and what are the different ways to define a string literal? **Answer:** Strings are created using single quotes (`'...'`), double quotes (`"..."`), or triple quotes (`'''...'''` or `"""..."""`). Triple quotes are used for multi-line strings.
2. **Question:** How do you access individual characters in a string using indexing? **Answer:** Use square brackets `[]` with the index of the character. Indexing starts from 0. Example: `my_string[0]` accesses the first character.
3. **Question:** Explain how to use negative indexing to access characters from the end of a string. **Answer:** Negative indexing starts from -1 for the last character. Example: `my_string[-1]` accesses the last character.
4. **Question:** What is string concatenation, and how do you perform it in Python? **Answer:** String concatenation is joining two or more strings. Use the + operator. Example: `"Hello" + " World"`.
5. **Question:** How do you repeat a string multiple times using the repetition operator? **Answer:** Use the * operator. Example: `"abc" * 3` results in `"abcabcabc"`.
6. **Question:** Explain string slicing and how to extract a substring from a string. **Answer:** String slicing extracts a portion of a string. Use `[start:end:step]`. Example: `my_string[1:5]` extracts characters from index 1 to 4.
7. **Question:** What happens if the slicing indices are out of range? **Answer:** Python handles it gracefully. If the start index is out of range, it starts from the beginning. If the end index is out of range, it goes to the end of the string.
8. **Question:** Are strings mutable or immutable in Python? Explain. **Answer:** Strings are immutable, meaning their contents cannot be changed after creation. Any operation that seems to modify a string actually creates a new [1] string.
9. **Question:** How do you find the length of a string in Python? **Answer:** Use the built-in `len()` function. Example: `len("Python")` returns 6.
10. **Question:** What is an escape sequence in a string, and provide an example? **Answer:** An escape sequence represents special characters. Example: `\n` for newline, `\t` for tab.

String Methods

11. **Question:** Explain the purpose of the `upper()` and `lower()` string methods and provide examples. **Answer:** `upper()` converts a string to uppercase, and `lower()` converts it to lowercase. Example: `"Hello".upper()` returns `"HELLO"`.
12. **Question:** What does the `strip()` method do, and how is it used to remove whitespace? **Answer:** `strip()` removes leading and trailing whitespace. Example: `" Python ".strip()` returns `"Python"`.
13. **Question:** How do you use the `split()` method to divide a string into a list of substrings? **Answer:** `split()` splits a string into a list based on a delimiter (default is whitespace). Example: `"apple,banana,orange".split(",")`.

14. **Question:** Explain the `replace()` method and how to substitute substrings within a string. **Answer:** `replace()` replaces all occurrences of a substring with another substring. Example: `"Hello World".replace("World", "Python")`.
15. **Question:** How can you check if a substring exists within a string using the `in` operator? **Answer:** Use the `in` operator. Example: `"apple" in "pineapple"` returns `True`.
16. **Question:** How do you find the index of the first occurrence of a substring using the `find()` method? **Answer:** `find()` returns the index of the first occurrence, or -1 if not found. Example: `"Python".find("th")` returns 2.
17. **Question:** What is the difference between `find()` and `index()` methods? **Answer:** `find()` returns -1 if the substring is not found, while `index()` raises a `ValueError`.
18. **Question:** How do you check if a string starts or ends with a specific substring using `startswith()` and `endswith()`? **Answer:** Use `startswith()` and `endswith()`. Example: `"Python".startswith("Py")` returns `True`.
19. **Question:** How do you join a list of strings into a single string using the `join()` method? **Answer:** Use `join()` with a separator string. Example: `", ".join(["apple", "banana", "orange"])`.
20. **Question:** How do you check if a string consists only of alphabetic characters using `isalpha()`? **Answer:** Use `isalpha()`. Example: `"Hello".isalpha()` returns `True`.
21. **Question:** How do you check if a string consists only of numeric characters using `isdigit()`? **Answer:** Use `isdigit()`. Example: `"123".isdigit()` returns `True`.
22. **Question:** How do you check if a string consists only of alphanumeric characters using `isalnum()`? **Answer:** Use `isalnum()`. Example: `"Hello123".isalnum()` returns `True`.
23. **Question:** How can you use f-strings to embed variables directly into a string? **Answer:** Use f-strings: `name = "Alice"; print(f"Hello, {name}!")`.
24. **Question:** How do you convert a string to a list of characters? **Answer:** Use the `list()` function. Example: `list("Python")` returns `['P', 'y', 't', 'h', 'o', 'n']`.
25. **Question:** How do you use the `count()` method to find the number of times a substring appears in a string? **Answer:** Use the `count()` method. Example: `"banana".count("a")` returns 3.

Practical Examples with Output:

1. Creating and Accessing Strings

```
# Creating a string
```

```
str1 = "Hello, Python!"

# Accessing characters
print(str1[0])   # First character
print(str1[-1])  # Last character
```

Output:

```
H
!
```

2. Concatenation of Strings

```
str1 = "Hello"
str2 = "Python"
result = str1 + " " + str2
print(result)
```

Output:

3. Repeating Strings

```
str1 = "Python"
result = str1 * 3
print(result)
```

Output:

```
PythonPythonPython
```

4. Slicing a String

```
str1 = "Hello, Python!"
substring = str1[7:13]
print(substring)
```

Output:

```
Python
```

5. Using upper() Method

```
str1 = "hello"
print(str1.upper())
```

Output:

```
HELLO
```

6. Using `lower()` Method

```
str1 = "HELLO"
print(str1.lower())
```

Output:

```
hello
```

7. Using `strip()` Method

```
str1 = "   Python is great!    "
print(str1.strip())
```

Output:

```
Python is great!
```

8. Using `split()` Method

```
str1 = "Python is easy"
words = str1.split()
print(words)
```

Output:

```
['Python', 'is', 'easy']
```

9. Using `replace()` Method

```
str1 = "I love Python"
new_str = str1.replace("Python", "Java")
print(new_str)
```

Output:

```
I love Java
```

10. Reversing a String using Slicing

```python
def reverse_string(s):
    return s[::-1]

str1 = "Python"
print(reverse_string(str1))
```

Output:

```
nohtyP
```

11. Counting Vowels in a String

```python
def count_vowels(s):
    vowels = "aeiouAEIOU"
    count = 0
    for char in s:
        if char in vowels:
            count += 1
    return count

str1 = "Hello, World!"
print(count_vowels(str1))
```

Output:

```
3
```

12. Accessing a Substring using Negative Indexing

```python
str1 = "Hello, Python!"
substring = str1[-7:-1]
print(substring)
```

Output:

```
Python
```

13. Using `find()` Method to Locate a Substring

```python
str1 = "I love Python programming"
position = str1.find("Python")
print(position)
```

Output:

```
7
```

14. Checking if a Substring Exists

```
str1 = "Python is amazing!"
result = "Python" in str1
print(result)
```

Output:

```
True
```

15. Combining String with Numbers

```
str1 = "The total cost is: "
cost = 150
result = str1 + str(cost)
print(result)
```

Output:

```
The total cost is: 150
```

CHAPTER 6: LISTS AND TUPLES

Introduction to Lists

A **list** in Python is an ordered collection of items that can hold different types of data such as numbers, strings, and other objects. Lists are **mutable**, meaning you can modify their contents after they are created. Lists are defined by placing items within square brackets `[]` and separating them with commas.

Creating and Accessing List Elements

Creating a List:

You can create a list by placing the elements in square brackets, separated by commas.

```
# Creating a list
fruits = ["apple", "banana", "cherry"]
```

Accessing List Elements:

You can access list elements using their index (starting from 0 for the first element).

```
# Accessing elements of a list
print(fruits[0])   # First element
print(fruits[2])   # Third element
```

Output:

```
apple
cherry
```

Negative Indexing:

In Python, you can also access elements using negative indices. Negative indices count from the end of the list (e.g., -1 is the last element).

```
print(fruits[-1])   # Last element
print(fruits[-2])   # Second last element
```

Output:

```
cherry
banana
```

List Methods

Python provides several methods to modify and manipulate lists. Below are some commonly used list methods:

1. **append()**: Adds an item to the end of the list.

```
fruits.append("orange")
print(fruits)
```

Output:

```
['apple', 'banana', 'cherry', 'orange']
```

2. **extend()**: Adds all elements of an iterable (e.g., another list) to the end of the current list.

```
fruits.extend(["grapes", "pineapple"])
print(fruits)
```

Output:

```
['apple', 'banana', 'cherry', 'orange', 'grapes', 'pineapple']
```

3. **remove()**: Removes the first occurrence of the specified element from the list.

```
fruits.remove("banana")
print(fruits)
```

Output:

```
['apple', 'cherry', 'orange', 'grapes', 'pineapple']
```

4. **sort()**: Sorts the list in ascending order by default.

```
fruits.sort()
print(fruits)
```

Output:

```
['apple', 'cherry', 'grapes', 'orange', 'pineapple']
```

Introduction to Tuples

A **tuple** is similar to a list but it is **immutable**, meaning once created, you cannot modify its elements. Tuples are defined using parentheses ().

```
# Creating a tuple
```

```
subjects = ("Math", "Physics", "Chemistry")
```

In Python, **Lists** and **Tuples** are both used to store collections of data. Although they appear similar, there are several key differences between them in terms of their properties, syntax, performance, and typical use cases.

Here's a detailed breakdown of the key differences between **Lists** and **Tuples**:

1. Syntax:

- **List:**
  - ○ A list is defined using **square brackets** [].
  - ○ It can contain any type of data (e.g., integers, strings, other lists, etc.).

  Example:

  ```
  my_list = [1, 2, 3, "apple", True]
  ```

- **Tuple:**
  - ○ A tuple is defined using **parentheses** ().
  - ○ Like lists, tuples can also store various types of data, but the key distinction is the syntax and immutability.

  Example:

  ```
  my_tuple = (1, 2, 3, "apple", True)
  ```

2. Mutability (Can it be changed?):

- **List:**
  - ○ **Mutable**: Lists can be modified after their creation. You can change their elements, add new items, or remove items.
  - ○ Example: You can modify an element, add items, or delete items.

  Example (Modifying a List):

  ```
  my_list = [1, 2, 3]
  my_list[0] = 10  # Modifying the first element
  my_list.append(4)  # Adding a new element
  my_list.remove(2)  # Removing an element
  print(my_list)  # Output: [10, 3, 4]
  ```

- **Tuple:**
  - **Immutable**: Once a tuple is created, it cannot be changed. You cannot modify, add, or remove elements from a tuple.
  - Example: Any attempt to modify a tuple will result in an error.

Example (Attempt to Modify a Tuple):

```
my_tuple = (1, 2, 3)
# The following will raise an error:
# my_tuple[0] = 10  # TypeError: 'tuple' object does not support
item assignment
```

3. Methods:

- **List:**
  - Lists have a variety of built-in methods that allow you to modify the list. Some commonly used methods include:
    - `append()`: Adds an element to the end of the list.
    - `remove()`: Removes the first occurrence of a specified element.
    - `sort()`: Sorts the elements of the list in ascending order.
    - `extend()`: Adds all elements from another iterable to the list.
    - `insert()`: Inserts an element at a specified position in the list.

Example (List Methods):

```
my_list = [5, 3, 8]
my_list.append(10)   # Adds 10 to the list
my_list.remove(3)    # Removes the first occurrence of 3
my_list.sort()       # Sorts the list
print(my_list)  # Output: [5, 8, 10]
```

- **Tuple:**
  - Tuples have fewer built-in methods because of their immutability. Some common methods include:
    - `count()`: Returns the number of occurrences of a specific element.
    - `index()`: Returns the index of the first occurrence of a specific element.

Example (Tuple Methods):

```
my_tuple = (1, 2, 3, 1)
print(my_tuple.count(1))  # Output: 2 (occurrences of 1)
print(my_tuple.index(3))  # Output: 2 (index of the first
occurrence of 3)
```

4. Performance:

- **List:**
  - Because lists are **mutable**, Python needs to allocate additional memory and manage the flexibility of changing their size and elements. This can make **lists slower** for operations compared to tuples.

    Example:

  - Lists generally take more time for operations like appending, removing elements, or modifying elements.
- **Tuple:**
  - **Immutable** objects are more efficient in terms of memory usage and performance. Because the size and elements of a tuple cannot change, Python can optimize its internal memory management, leading to **faster access and performance**.

    Example:

  - Operations like iteration and lookup are faster in tuples because Python doesn't need to manage the mutable nature of the object.

---

5. Use Case:

- **List:**
  - Use a **list** when you need a **mutable** collection of items, meaning the data might change during the execution of the program.
  - Common use cases:
    - Storing elements that may be modified.
    - Keeping track of data where elements will be added or removed.

    Example Use Case:

  - Storing items in a shopping cart, where the user can add or remove products.
- **Tuple:**
  - Use a **tuple** when you need an **immutable** collection of items, meaning the data will remain constant throughout the program.
  - Common use cases:
    - Storing fixed data, like coordinates or RGB values.
    - Returning multiple values from a function (tuples are often used as function return types).
    - Using tuples as dictionary keys (since tuples are hashable, they can be used as keys in dictionaries, unlike lists).

Example Use Case:

    o Storing the fixed configuration settings of an application, like the default color or position.

Summary of Differences:

Feature	List	Tuple
Syntax	Defined using square brackets []	Defined using parentheses ()
Mutability	Mutable (can be changed)	Immutable (cannot be changed)
Methods	Rich set of methods (e.g., append, remove, sort)	Fewer methods (e.g., count, index)
Performance	Slower due to mutability	Faster due to immutability
Use Case	When data is expected to change	When data is constant or fixed
Memory Usage	Requires more memory due to flexibility	Requires less memory due to immutability

---

Tuple Operations

1. **Accessing Elements:**

Just like lists, you can access tuple elements using indexing.

```
# Accessing tuple elements
print(subjects[0])   # First element
```

Output:

```
Math
```

2. **Concatenation:**

You can concatenate two tuples to create a new one.

```
new_subjects = subjects + ("Biology", "English")
print(new_subjects)
```

Output:

```
('Math', 'Physics', 'Chemistry', 'Biology', 'English')
```

3. **Repetition:**

Tuples can be repeated using the * operator.

```
repeat_subjects = subjects * 2
print(repeat_subjects)
```

Output:

```
('Math', 'Physics', 'Chemistry', 'Math', 'Physics', 'Chemistry')
```

MCQ

1. Which of the following is the correct syntax to create an empty list in Python?

a) `[]`
b) `()`
c) `{}`
d) `list()`

Answer: a) `[]`

2. What will be the output of the following code?

```
fruits = ["apple", "banana", "cherry"]
fruits.append("orange")
print(fruits)
```

a) `['apple', 'banana', 'cherry', 'orange']`
b) `['apple', 'orange', 'banana', 'cherry']`
c) `['orange', 'banana', 'cherry']`
d) `['apple', 'banana', 'cherry']`

Answer: a) `['apple', 'banana', 'cherry', 'orange']`

3. Which of the following methods is used to remove a specific element from a list?

a) `pop()`
b) `delete()`
c) `remove()`
d) `discard()`

Answer: c) `remove()`

4. What does the `extend()` method do in a list?

a) Adds a single element to the list
b) Adds multiple elements to the list
c) Removes elements from the list
d) Sorts the list

Answer: b) Adds multiple elements to the list

5. What is the default return value of the `append()` method?

a) The added element
b) The modified list
c) `None`
d) `False`

Answer: c) `None`

6. Which method is used to find the index of an element in a list?

a) `search()`
b) `locate()`
c) `find()`
d) `index()`

Answer: d) `index()`

7. What will be the output of the following code?

```
numbers = [1, 2, 3, 4, 5]
numbers.sort(reverse=True)
print(numbers)
```

a) `[5, 4, 3, 2, 1]`
b) `[1, 2, 3, 4, 5]`
c) `[4, 3, 2, 1, 5]`
d) `[5, 4, 3, 2, 1, 6]`

Answer: a) `[5, 4, 3, 2, 1]`

8. Which of the following is true about tuples?

a) Tuples are mutable
b) Tuples are immutable
c) Tuples can contain only integers
d) Tuples can only contain strings

Answer: b) Tuples are immutable

9. What will be the output of the following code?

```
a = (1, 2, 3, 4)
b = (5, 6)
c = a + b
print(c)
```

a) `(1, 2, 3, 4, 5, 6)`
b) `(1, 2, 3, 4, 5)`
c) `(5, 6, 1, 2, 3, 4)`
d) Error: Cannot concatenate tuples

Answer: a) `(1, 2, 3, 4, 5, 6)`

10. Which of the following is the correct way to access the first element of a tuple `my_tuple = (1, 2, 3)`?

a) `my_tuple[0]`
b) `my_tuple(0)`

c) `my_tuple.first()`
d) `my_tuple[1]`

Answer: a) `my_tuple[0]`

---

11. Which of the following methods is used to remove an item from a list at a specified index?

a) `remove()`
b) `pop()`
c) `delete()`
d) `discard()`

Answer: b) `pop()`

---

12. What does the following code do?

```
numbers = [1, 2, 3, 4, 5]
numbers.pop(2)
print(numbers)
```

a) Removes the element at index 2
b) Removes the element at index 3
c) Removes the first element
d) Removes the last element

Answer: a) Removes the element at index 2

---

13. How do you create a tuple containing only one element?

a) `tuple = (1)`
b) `tuple = (1,)`
c) `tuple = [1]`
d) `tuple = 1`

Answer: b) `tuple = (1,)`

---

14. Which of the following operations cannot be performed on a tuple?

a) Iterating through its elements
b) Accessing an element by index
c) Appending an element
d) Concatenating tuples

Answer: c) Appending an element

---

15. What will be the output of the following code?

```
a = [10, 20, 30]
b = a
b.append(40)
print(a)
```

a) `[10, 20, 30]`
b) `[10, 20, 30, 40]`
c) `[40, 10, 20, 30]`
d) `[20, 30, 40]`

Answer: b) `[10, 20, 30, 40]`

---

16. Which method is used to reverse the elements of a list in Python?

a) `flip()`
b) `reverse()`
c) `reverse_elements()`
d) `reversed()`

Answer: b) `reverse()`

---

17. Which of the following is the correct syntax to access the last element of a tuple `my_tuple = (1, 2, 3)`?

a) `my_tuple[-1]`
b) `my_tuple[0]`
c) `my_tuple[3]`
d) `my_tuple.last()`

Answer: a) `my_tuple[-1]`

18. What will be the output of the following code?

```
numbers = [5, 3, 8, 6]
numbers.sort()
print(numbers)
```

a) `[8, 6, 5, 3]`
b) `[3, 5, 6, 8]`
c) `[5, 3, 6, 8]`
d) `[6, 8, 3, 5]`

Answer: b) `[3, 5, 6, 8]`

19. Which method is used to remove all elements from a list?

a) `clear()`
b) `delete()`
c) `remove_all()`
d) `reset()`

Answer: a) `clear()`

20. What will be the output of the following code?

```
a = (1, 2, 3)
b = a * 2
print(b)
```

a) `(1, 2, 3, 1, 2, 3)`
b) `(2, 4, 6)`
c) `[(1, 2, 3), (1, 2, 3)]`
d) `Error`

Answer: a) `(1, 2, 3, 1, 2, 3)`

25 medium-sized questions and answers covering Introduction to Lists and Tuples in Python:

Introduction to Lists

1. **Question:** How do you create a list in Python, and what types of elements can it contain? **Answer:** Lists are created using square brackets `[]` and can contain elements of any data type, including other lists. Example: `my_list = [1, "hello", 3.14]`.
2. **Question:** How do you access elements in a list using indexing? **Answer:** Use square brackets `[]` with the index of the element. Indexing starts from 0. Example: `my_list[0]` accesses the first element.
3. **Question:** Explain how to use negative indexing to access elements from the end of a list. **Answer:** Negative indexing starts from -1 for the last element. Example: `my_list[-1]` accesses the last element.
4. **Question:** How do you slice a list to extract a sublist? **Answer:** Use `[start:end:step]` notation. Example: `my_list[1:3]` extracts elements from index 1 to 2.
5. **Question:** Are lists mutable or immutable in Python? Explain. **Answer:** Lists are mutable, meaning their elements can be changed after creation.
6. **Question:** How do you add an element to the end of a list using the `append()` method? **Answer:** Use `list_name.append(element)`. Example: `my_list.append(4)`.
7. **Question:** Explain the difference between `append()` and `extend()` methods. **Answer:** `append()` adds a single element to the end, while `extend()` adds all elements from an iterable (like another list) to the end.
8. **Question:** How do you remove an element from a list using the `remove()` method? **Answer:** Use `list_name.remove(element)`. It removes the first occurrence of the specified element.
9. **Question:** How do you sort a list in ascending order using the `sort()` method? **Answer:** Use `list_name.sort()`. This modifies the list in place.
10. **Question:** How do you insert an element at a specific index in a list? **Answer:** Use `list_name.insert(index, element)`.
11. **Question:** How to remove an element from a list, by index? **Answer:** Use `list_name.pop(index)`. If no index is provided, it removes and returns the last element.
12. **Question:** How do you find the length of a list in Python? **Answer:** Use the built-in `len()` function. Example: `len(my_list)`.
13. **Question:** How do you check if an element exists in a list? **Answer:** Use the `in` operator. Example: `if element in my_list:`.

Introduction to Tuples

14. **Question:** How do you create a tuple in Python, and what are the key differences between lists and tuples? **Answer:** Tuples are created using parentheses `()` and are immutable, unlike lists. Example: `my_tuple = (1, "hello", 3.14)`.

15. **Question:** Explain the immutability of tuples and why it is important. **Answer:** Immutability means tuple elements cannot be changed after creation. It's important for data integrity and when tuples are used as keys in dictionaries.
16. **Question:** How do you access elements in a tuple using indexing and slicing? **Answer:** Same as lists: `my_tuple[0]` for indexing, `my_tuple[1:3]` for slicing.
17. **Question:** What happens if you try to modify an element in a tuple? **Answer:** Python raises a `TypeError` because tuples are immutable.
18. **Question:** How do you concatenate two tuples in Python? **Answer:** Use the + operator. Example: `tuple1 + tuple2`.
19. **Question:** How do you repeat a tuple multiple times using the repetition operator? **Answer:** Use the * operator. Example: `my_tuple * 3`.
20. **Question:** How do you unpack a tuple into individual variables? **Answer:** Assign the tuple to a set of variables. Example: `a, b, c = my_tuple`.
21. **Question:** When would you use a tuple instead of a list in Python? **Answer:** When you need an immutable sequence or when using tuples as keys in dictionaries.
22. **Question:** How do you find the index of an element in a tuple? **Answer:** Use the `index()` method. Example: `my_tuple.index(element)`.
23. **Question:** How do you count the occurrences of an element in a tuple? **Answer:** Use the `count()` method. Example: `my_tuple.count(element)`.
24. **Question:** How can you convert a list to a tuple and vice versa? **Answer:** Use `tuple()` and `list()` functions. Example: `my_tuple = tuple(my_list)`, `my_list = list(my_tuple)`.
25. **Question:** How to create a tuple with a single element? **Answer:** Add a trailing comma. Example: `single_tuple = (5,)`. Without the comma, it would be interpreted as a regular expression.

Practical Examples

---

1. Find the Maximum, Minimum, and Average of Numbers in a List

This example demonstrates how to use lists to calculate the maximum, minimum, and average of numbers.

```
# List of numbers
numbers = [15, 20, 5, 10, 25, 30, 35]

# Finding the maximum, minimum, and average
max_num = max(numbers)
min_num = min(numbers)
avg_num = sum(numbers) / len(numbers)

print("Maximum:", max_num)
```

```
print("Minimum:", min_num)
print("Average:", avg_num)
```

Output:

```
Maximum: 35
Minimum: 5
Average: 20.0
```

Explanation:

- `max(numbers)` returns the maximum value from the list.
- `min(numbers)` returns the minimum value.
- `sum(numbers) / len(numbers)` calculates the average by dividing the sum of the elements by the length of the list.

2. Create a Tuple of Subjects in a Semester

This example demonstrates how to create and manipulate a tuple containing subjects for a semester.

```
# Creating a tuple of subjects
semester_subjects = ("Math", "Physics", "Chemistry", "English")

# Accessing elements of the tuple
print("First subject:", semester_subjects[0])

# Concatenating another tuple
semester_subjects = semester_subjects + ("Biology", "History")
print("Updated subjects:", semester_subjects)

# Repeating the tuple
repeated_subjects = semester_subjects * 2
print("Repeated subjects:", repeated_subjects)
```

Output:

```
First subject: Math
Updated subjects: ('Math', 'Physics', 'Chemistry', 'English',
'Biology', 'History')
Repeated subjects: ('Math', 'Physics', 'Chemistry', 'English',
'Biology', 'History', 'Math', 'Physics', 'Chemistry', 'English',
'Biology', 'History')
```

Explanation:

- You can access elements of a tuple just like a list, using an index.
- You can concatenate tuples and repeat them using the + and * operators.

3. Adding and Removing Elements from a List

This example demonstrates how to add elements to a list using `append()` and `insert()`, and remove elements using `remove()` and `pop()`.

```
# Creating a list
fruits = ["apple", "banana", "cherry"]

# Adding elements
fruits.append("orange")   # Adds 'orange' to the end
fruits.insert(1, "grapes")   # Adds 'grapes' at index 1

# Removing elements
fruits.remove("banana")   # Removes 'banana' from the list
removed_item = fruits.pop()   # Removes the last item and returns it

print("Updated Fruits List:", fruits)
print("Removed Item:", removed_item)
```

Output:

```
Updated Fruits List: ['apple', 'grapes', 'cherry', 'orange']
Removed Item: orange
```

Explanation:

- `append()` adds an item to the end of the list.
- `insert()` adds an item at a specific index.
- `remove()` deletes the first occurrence of a specified element.
- `pop()` removes and returns the last element of the list.

---

4. Count Occurrences of an Element in a List

This example shows how to count the number of occurrences of an element in a list using the `count()` method.

```
# List with repeated elements
numbers = [1, 2, 3, 1, 4, 1, 5]

# Counting occurrences of the number 1
count_ones = numbers.count(1)

print("Number of times 1 appears:", count_ones)
```

Output:

```
Number of times 1 appears: 3
```

Explanation:

- The count() method returns the number of occurrences of the specified element in the list.

5. Slicing a List

This example demonstrates how to extract portions of a list using slicing.

```python
# List of numbers
numbers = [1, 2, 3, 4, 5, 6, 7, 8, 9, 10]

# Slicing the list
first_five = numbers[:5]   # Elements from index 0 to 4
last_three = numbers[-3:]   # Last three elements

print("First five elements:", first_five)
print("Last three elements:", last_three)
```

Output:

```
First five elements: [1, 2, 3, 4, 5]
Last three elements: [8, 9, 10]
```

Explanation:

- The slicing syntax list[start:end] is used to extract a portion of the list.
- [:5] selects the first five elements, and [-3:] selects the last three elements.

6. Nested List and Accessing Elements

This example demonstrates how to work with nested lists (lists inside lists).

```python
# Nested list
matrix = [[1, 2, 3], [4, 5, 6], [7, 8, 9]]

# Accessing elements in a nested list
first_element = matrix[0][0]   # Accessing first element of the first sublist
last_element = matrix[2][2]    # Accessing last element of the last sublist

print("First element:", first_element)
print("Last element:", last_element)
```

Output:

```
First element: 1
Last element: 9
```

Explanation:

- In a nested list, elements are accessed using two indices: the first for the sublist and the second for the element within that sublist.

---

7. Tuple Packing and Unpacking

This example shows how to pack and unpack tuples.

```
# Packing values into a tuple
person = ("John", 25, "Engineer")

# Unpacking the tuple into variables
name, age, profession = person

print("Name:", name)
print("Age:", age)
print("Profession:", profession)
```

Output:

```
Name: John
Age: 25
Profession: Engineer
```

Explanation:

- **Packing** is when multiple values are grouped into a tuple.
- **Unpacking** is when the tuple values are assigned to variables.

---

8. Iterating Over a List Using a For Loop

This example shows how to iterate over the elements of a list using a `for` loop.

```
# List of numbers
numbers = [2, 4, 6, 8, 10]

# Iterating through the list
for num in numbers:
    print("Number:", num)
```

Output:

```
Number: 2
Number: 4
Number: 6
Number: 8
Number: 10
```

Explanation:

- A `for` loop is used to iterate over each item in the list and print it.

9. Tuple Concatenation

This example demonstrates how to concatenate two tuples to create a new tuple.

```
# Two tuples
tuple1 = (1, 2, 3)
tuple2 = (4, 5, 6)

# Concatenating tuples
combined_tuple = tuple1 + tuple2

print("Concatenated Tuple:", combined_tuple)
```

Output:

```
Concatenated Tuple: (1, 2, 3, 4, 5, 6)
```

Explanation:

- Tuples are immutable, but you can concatenate two tuples using the + operator to create a new tuple.

10. Tuple Unpacking with Swapping Values

This example demonstrates how to swap two variables using tuple unpacking.

```
# Variables to swap
a = 10
b = 20

# Swapping values using tuple unpacking
a, b = b, a

print("Swapped values: a =", a, ", b =", b)
```

Output:

```
Swapped values: a = 20 , b = 10
```

Explanation:

- Tuple unpacking allows you to swap two values in a single line of code without using a temporary variable.

---

11. Find Index of an Element in a List

This example demonstrates how to find the index of an element in a list using the `index()` method.

```
# List of items
fruits = ["apple", "banana", "cherry", "orange"]

# Finding index of 'cherry'
index_of_cherry = fruits.index("cherry")

print("Index of 'cherry':", index_of_cherry)
```

Output:

```
Index of 'cherry': 2
```

Explanation:

- The `index()` method returns the index of the first occurrence of the specified element.

---

12. Reversing a List

This example shows how to reverse the order of elements in a list.

```
# List of numbers
numbers = [1, 2, 3, 4, 5]

# Reversing the list
numbers.reverse()

print("Reversed List:", numbers)
```

Output:

```
Reversed List: [5, 4, 3, 2, 1]
```

Explanation:

- The `reverse()` method reverses the elements of the list in place.

CHAPTER 7: FILE HANDLING BASICS

File handling in Python allows you to store, retrieve, and manipulate data that persists beyond the duration of a program's execution. It is a crucial part of programming, as many applications require working with data stored in files, such as logs, user inputs, configurations, and databases.

Introduction to File Handling

Importance of File Handling:

File handling is vital for persistent storage and retrieval of data. It allows you to save information from a program for later use, share data between different applications, and keep records of program outputs, logs, or configurations.

Python's built-in `open()` function enables interaction with files on the system, and through it, you can perform tasks such as reading, writing, and updating files. Files may be text files (e.g., `.txt`) or binary files (e.g., `.jpg`, `.exe`), and handling them requires understanding file modes, file operations, and file closing.

Opening, Reading, Writing, and Closing Files

1. **Opening Files:**
   - The `open()` function is used to open a file. This function takes two arguments:
     - **Filename** (path to the file to be opened)
     - **Mode** (optional, defines the file's access mode)

   Syntax:

   ```
   file = open("filename.txt", "r")   # Open in read mode
   ```

   Common file access modes:

   - **"r"**: Read (default mode, opens the file for reading).
   - **"w"**: Write (creates a new file or truncates an existing file).
   - **"a"**: Append (opens the file for appending data to the end).
   - **"b"**: Binary (used with other modes for reading or writing binary files).
   - **"x"**: Exclusive creation (creates a new file, but raises an error if it exists).
2. **Reading Files:**
   - `read()`: Reads the entire file content.
   - `readline()`: Reads one line from the file.
   - `readlines()`: Reads all lines from the file into a list.

Example:

```
file = open("file.txt", "r")
content = file.read()  # Reads the entire file content
print(content)
file.close()
```

3. **Writing to Files:**
   o **write()**: Writes a string to the file.
   o **writelines()**: Writes a list of strings to the file.

Example:

```
file = open("output.txt", "w")
file.write("Hello, World!\n")  # Writes a string to the file
file.close()
```

4. **Closing Files:**
   o Always close files after performing operations using **close()** to free up system resources.

Example:

```
file = open("file.txt", "r")
content = file.read()
file.close()  # Ensure to close the file after use
```

Simple File Operations

1. **Write to a File:** To write to a file, you open the file in write ("w") or append ("a") mode. Writing in "w" mode overwrites the content of the file, while "a" mode appends data at the end.

   Example of writing:

```
file = open("student_names.txt", "w")
file.write("Alice\nBob\nCharlie\n")
file.close()
```

   In this example, a file named student_names.txt is created, and the names Alice, Bob, and Charlie are written to it. Each name is followed by a newline character (\n).

2. **Read from a File:** After writing to the file, you can read the file content. Use the **open()** function in "r" mode to open the file for reading.

Example of reading:

```
file = open("student_names.txt", "r")
content = file.read()   # Reads the entire file content
print(content)
file.close()
```

This will output:

```
Alice
Bob
Charlie
```

Practical Examples

1. **Store Student Names and Retrieve Them from a File:**

   This practical example demonstrates how to write a list of student names to a file and then retrieve them.

   Step 1: Write student names to a file.

   ```
   def write_student_names():
       # Open the file in write mode
       with open("students.txt", "w") as file:
           # Writing student names to the file
           file.write("John\n")
           file.write("Emma\n")
           file.write("Sophia\n")
           file.write("James\n")

       print("Student names have been written to the file.")

   write_student_names()   # Call function to write names
   ```

   Step 2: Read student names from the file.

   ```
   def read_student_names():
       # Open the file in read mode
       with open("students.txt", "r") as file:
           # Reading the entire content
           students = file.read().splitlines()
           return students

       # Closing is automatically handled by 'with' statement.

   student_names = read_student_names()   # Call function to read
   names
   print("Student names retrieved from the file:", student_names)
   ```

Output:

```
Student names have been written to the file.
Student names retrieved from the file: ['John', 'Emma', 'Sophia',
'James']
```

Explanation:

- o The **write_student_names()** function opens the file students.txt in write mode and writes student names, each followed by a newline.
- o The **read_student_names()** function opens the file in read mode, retrieves the names using **read()**, and splits them into a list using **splitlines()**.
- o The **with open()** syntax automatically handles closing the file after use, making the code more efficient and cleaner.

Practical Example 1: Append Data to an Existing File

Appending data to a file means adding new content without modifying the existing data. This is useful when you need to log data or add entries to a file over time.

Example:

```
def append_to_file():
    # Open the file in append mode
    with open("log.txt", "a") as file:
        # Append a new log entry to the file
        file.write("New log entry: User login at 2024-12-22 10:30
AM\n")

    print("New log entry appended to the file.")

append_to_file()  # Call function to append data
```

Explanation:

- **open("log.txt", "a")**: Opens the file log.txt in append mode ("a"), which allows adding new content at the end without overwriting existing content.
- **file.write()**: Appends a new log entry to the file.

Output:

```
New log entry appended to the file.
```

Practical Example 2: Copy Contents from One File to Another

This example demonstrates how to copy the contents of one file to another file. This could be useful for backups or transferring data between files.

Example:

```python
def copy_file():
    # Open the source file in read mode
    with open("source.txt", "r") as source_file:
        content = source_file.read()  # Read content from the source
file

    # Open the destination file in write mode
    with open("destination.txt", "w") as destination_file:
        destination_file.write(content)  # Write the content to the
destination file

    print("Content copied from source.txt to destination.txt.")

copy_file()  # Call function to copy content
```

Explanation:

- **open("source.txt", "r")**: Opens the source file for reading.
- **read()**: Reads the entire content of the source file.
- **open("destination.txt", "w")**: Opens the destination file for writing and overwrites its contents.
- **write()**: Writes the content of the source file to the destination file.

Output:

```
Content copied from source.txt to destination.txt.
```

Practical Example 3: Counting the Number of Words in a File

This example reads a file, counts the number of words, and prints the count. This could be useful for analyzing text files.

Example:

```python
def count_words_in_file():
    # Open the file in read mode
    with open("text_file.txt", "r") as file:
        content = file.read()  # Read the entire file content
        words = content.split()  # Split the content into words
        word_count = len(words)  # Count the number of words
```

```
    print(f"Number of words in the file: {word_count}")

count_words_in_file()  # Call function to count words
```

Explanation:

- `split()`: Splits the file content into a list of words based on spaces.
- `len(words)`: Calculates the number of words in the list.

Output:

```
Number of words in the file: 58
```

Practical Example 4: Replace a Word in a File

This example shows how to search for a word in a file and replace it with another word. This can be used for text replacement tasks such as modifying content or correcting mistakes.

Example:

```
def replace_word_in_file():
    # Open the file in read mode
    with open("document.txt", "r") as file:
        content = file.read()  # Read the entire content

    # Replace the word "old" with "new"
    content = content.replace("old", "new")

    # Open the file in write mode to overwrite it with the updated
content
    with open("document.txt", "w") as file:
        file.write(content)  # Write the modified content back to the
file

    print("Word replaced successfully in the file.")

replace_word_in_file()  # Call function to replace word
```

Explanation:

- `replace("old", "new")`: This replaces every occurrence of the word "old" with "new" in the file content.
- `open("document.txt", "w")`: Reopens the file in write mode to overwrite the file with the modified content.

Output:

```
Word replaced successfully in the file.
```

MCQ

1. What is the primary purpose of file handling in Python?

A) To store variables temporarily
B) To manipulate data from external files
C) To create functions
D) To display messages on the screen

Answer: B) To manipulate data from external files

2. Which function is used to open a file in Python?

A) `open_file()`
B) `open()`
C) `file_open()`
D) `read()`

Answer: B) `open()`

3. What does the `r` mode in the `open()` function do?

A) Opens a file for writing only
B) Opens a file for reading only
C) Opens a file for appending
D) Opens a file for both reading and writing

Answer: B) Opens a file for reading only

4. Which of the following operations is not supported by the `open()` function?

A) Opening a file for reading
B) Opening a file for writing
C) Closing a file
D) Opening a file for appending

Answer: C) Closing a file

---

5. What is the correct syntax to read the entire content of a file?

A) `file.read()`
B) `file.open()`
C) `read(file)`
D) `file.readAll()`

Answer: A) `file.read()`

---

6. Which function is used to write to a file in Python?

A) `write()`
B) `writeline()`
C) `writefile()`
D) `open()`

Answer: A) `write()`

---

7. What happens if you try to read from a file opened in write-only mode?

A) The file is read successfully
B) Python will raise a `ValueError`
C) Python will raise an `IOError`
D) The program will crash without an error message

Answer: C) Python will raise an `IOError`

---

8. Which mode in `open()` function allows both reading and writing to a file?

A) `r`
B) `w`
C) `r+`
D) `a`

Answer: C) `r+`

---

9. How do you append data to a file in Python?

A) `open("file.txt", "r")`
B) `open("file.txt", "w")`
C) `open("file.txt", "a")`
D) `open("file.txt", "rw")`

Answer: C) `open("file.txt", "a")`

---

10. What does the `close()` function do in file handling?

A) It closes the file and saves changes
B) It clears the file content
C) It closes the file and discards any unsaved changes
D) It opens a new file for writing

Answer: A) It closes the file and saves changes

---

11. Which of the following is a valid way to read lines from a file in Python?

A) `file.readline()`
B) `file.readline()`
C) `file.read()`
D) `file.line()`

Answer: B) `file.readline()`

---

12. What is the default mode when opening a file using `open()`?

A) `r`
B) `w`
C) `rb`
D) `a`

Answer: A) `r`

---

13. What will happen if you try to open a file in write mode (`w`) that does not exist?

A) It will raise a `FileNotFoundError`
B) It will create a new file
C) It will return `None`
D) It will return a `TypeError`

Answer: B) It will create a new file

---

14. What is the use of the `with` statement in file handling?

A) To open and close the file automatically
B) To read the entire file in one go
C) To write to the file multiple times
D) To allow simultaneous file access

Answer: A) To open and close the file automatically

---

15. Which of the following functions will read all lines of a file into a list?

A) `file.readlines()`
B) `file.read()`
C) `file.readline()`
D) `file.readlines()`

Answer: D) `file.readlines()`

16. What does the `strip()` method do in Python?

A) Removes the last character of a string
B) Removes leading and trailing whitespace from a string
C) Converts the string to uppercase
D) Replaces spaces in a string with underscores

Answer: B) Removes leading and trailing whitespace from a string

---

17. Which of the following is used to write multiple lines to a file?

A) `file.writeline()`
B) `file.write()`
C) `file.writeall()`
D) `file.writelines()`

Answer: D) `file.writelines()`

---

18. Which file operation allows you to read data after writing to the file?

A) `w`
B) `r+`
C) `a`
D) `wb`

Answer: B) `r+`

---

19. Which of the following is true about the `write()` function in file handling?

A) It can write only one line at a time
B) It automatically adds a newline after each line
C) It requires manual management of newlines
D) It can only write strings

Answer: C) It requires manual management of newlines

---

20. What is the main difference between `open()` in write mode (w) and append mode (a)?

A) `w` overwrites the existing file, while `a` appends to it
B) Both overwrite the file
C) `w` appends, while `a` overwrites
D) There is no difference

Answer: A) `w` overwrites the existing file, while `a` appends to it

---

21. How would you read only the first line of a file?

A) `file.read(1)`
B) `file.readline()`
C) `file.readline(1)`
D) `file.firstline()`

Answer: B) `file.readline()`

---

22. Which of the following will open a file for reading and writing in binary mode?

A) `open('file.txt', 'r')`
B) `open('file.txt', 'rb')`
C) `open('file.txt', 'w')`
D) `open('file.txt', 'r+')`

Answer: B) `open('file.txt', 'rb')`

---

23. What will be the result of opening a file in 'a' mode if the file doesn't exist?

A) `FileNotFoundError`
B) The file will be created
C) An empty file will be returned
D) An error message will be displayed

Answer: B) The file will be created

138

24. What is the purpose of the `flush()` method in file handling?

A) To clear the file content
B) To write content to the file
C) To flush the file buffer to disk
D) To close the file

Answer: C) To flush the file buffer to disk

25. What will happen if you attempt to read from a file opened in write mode (`w`)?

A) The program will throw a `FileError`
B) The file content will be overwritten
C) Python will return an empty string
D) It will raise an `IOError`

Answer: D) It will raise an `IOError`

26. What does the `seek()` method do in file handling?

A) It searches for a specific word in the file
B) It moves the file pointer to a specified position
C) It writes data to a file
D) It closes the file

Answer: B) It moves the file pointer to a specified position

27. What is the return value of the `readline()` function?

A) A list of strings
B) A single line of the file
C) The entire file
D) The file pointer

Answer: B) A single line of the file

28. Which of the following file modes is used for binary file writing?

A) `w`
B) `wb`
C) `a`
D) `r+`

Answer: B) `wb`

29. Which method is used to check if the end of file (EOF) is reached during reading?

A) `file.eof()`
B) `file.end()`
C) `file.read()`
D) `file.tell()`

Answer: A) `file.eof()`

30. In file handling, which method is used to read one byte at a time from a file?

A) `file.read(1)`
B) `file.readline()`
C) `file.read()`
D) `file.next()`

Answer: A) `file.read(1)`

25 questions and answers covering Introduction to File Handling in Python:

Introduction to File Handling

1. **Question:** What is file handling in Python, and why is it important? **Answer:** File handling is the process of reading from and writing to files. It's important for persistent data storage, configuration management, and data exchange.
2. **Question:** What are the different modes for opening a file in Python, and what do they represent? **Answer:** Modes include: * `'r'` (read): Opens a file for reading (default). * `'w'` (write): Opens a file for writing, creates if it doesn't exist, truncates if it does. * `'a'` (append): Opens a file for appending, creates if it

doesn't exist. * `'x'` (exclusive creation): Creates a file, fails if it exists. * `'b'` (binary): Binary mode. * `'t'` (text): Text mode (default).

3. **Question:** How do you open a file in Python, and what is the syntax for the `open()` function? **Answer:** Use `open(filename, mode)`. Example: `file = open("myfile.txt", "r")`.

4. **Question:** How do you read the entire content of a file into a string? **Answer:** Use `file.read()`. Example: `content = file.read()`.

5. **Question:** How do you read a file line by line? **Answer:** Use `file.readline()` to read one line at a time or iterate over the file object directly: `for line in file:`.

6. **Question:** How do you write data to a file in Python? **Answer:** Use `file.write(data)`. Example: `file.write("Hello, world!")`.

7. **Question:** Why is it important to close a file after you're done with it, and how do you close a file? **Answer:** Closing a file releases system resources and ensures data is written to disk. Use `file.close()`.

8. **Question:** Explain the use of the `with` statement in file handling. **Answer:** The `with` statement automatically closes the file, even if exceptions occur. Example: `with open("myfile.txt", "r") as file:`.

9. **Question:** What happens if you try to open a file that doesn't exist in read mode? **Answer:** Python raises a `FileNotFoundError`.

10. **Question:** How do you check if a file exists before attempting to open it? **Answer:** Use the `os.path.exists()` function from the `os` module.

Simple File Operations

11. **Question:** Write a Python code snippet to create a new file and write some text to it. **Answer:**

```python
with open("newfile.txt", "w") as file:
    file.write("This is a new file.")
```

12. **Question:** How do you append data to an existing file without overwriting its content? **Answer:** Open the file in append mode (`"a"`) and use `file.write()`.

13. **Question:** Write a Python code snippet to read the first line of a file. **Answer:**

```python
with open("myfile.txt", "r") as file:
    first_line = file.readline()
    print(first_line)
```

14. **Question:** How do you read all lines of a file into a list? **Answer:** Use `file.readlines()`. Example: `lines = file.readlines()`.

15. **Question:** How to remove the newline character from the end of each line when reading from a file? **Answer:** Use `line.strip()` when iterating through the file.

16. **Question:** How do you write a list of strings to a file, with each string on a new line? **Answer:**

```python
lines = ["Line 1", "Line 2", "Line 3"]
```

```
with open("output.txt", "w") as file:
    for line in lines:
        file.write(line + "\n")
```

17. **Question:** How do you read a file and count the number of lines? **Answer:**

```
with open("myfile.txt", "r") as file:
    line_count = len(file.readlines())
    print(line_count)
```

18. **Question:** How can you write numerical data to a file and read it back as numerical data? **Answer:** Convert numbers to strings for writing and convert back to numbers when reading.
19. **Question:** How do you handle exceptions that might occur during file operations? **Answer:** Use `try-except` blocks. Example: `try: ... except FileNotFoundError: ...`.
20. **Question:** How to check if a file is empty? **Answer:** Check if `os.path.getsize(filename)` returns 0.
21. **Question:** How do you read a file character by character? **Answer:** Use `file.read(1)` in a loop.
22. **Question:** How do you create a backup of a file before modifying it? **Answer:** Use `shutil.copyfile()` from the `shutil` module.
23. **Question:** How do you move a file to a different directory using Python? **Answer:** Use `shutil.move()` from the `shutil` module.
24. **Question:** How do you delete a file using python code? **Answer:** Use `os.remove(filename)` from the `os` module.
25. **Question:** How to read a csv file, and store the data in a list of lists? **Answer:** Use the csv module.

```
data = []
with open('my_file.csv', 'r') as file:
    csv_reader = csv.reader(file)
    for row in csv_reader:
        data.append(row)
```

practical questions and answers on File Handling in Python:

1. Question: You have a large dataset generated by a sensor that you need to store for later analysis. How would you use Python to save this data to a file?

Answer: I would open a file in write ('w') or append ('a') mode, depending on whether I want to overwrite or add to existing data. Then, I would format the sensor data (e.g., as comma-separated values or JSON) and write it to the file using `file.write()`. Finally, I would close the file using `file.close()` or use a `with` statement to ensure it's closed automatically.

2. Question: You need to read a configuration file that contains settings for your application. How would you use Python to read this file and extract the settings?

Answer: I would open the configuration file in read ('r') mode. Then, I would read the file line by line using `file.readline()` or `file.readlines()`. I would parse each line to extract the settings (e.g., key-value pairs) and store them in a dictionary or other suitable data structure. Finally, I would close the file.

3. Question: You have a log file that you need to analyze to find specific error messages. How would you use Python to read the file and search for these messages?

Answer: I would open the log file in read ('r') mode. Then, I would iterate through the file line by line. For each line, I would check if it contains the error messages I'm looking for using string methods like `in` or `find()`. If a match is found, I would extract the relevant information and store it.

4. Question: You want to create a script that backs up a file by copying its contents to a new file with a timestamp in the filename. How would you achieve this?

Answer: I would use the `shutil` module to copy the file. First, I'd get the current timestamp using the `datetime` module. Then, I'd create the new filename with the timestamp and use `shutil.copyfile(original_file, new_file)` to copy the contents.

5. Question: You need to write a script that reads a text file and counts the number of words in it. How would you implement this?

Answer: I would open the file in read ('r') mode. Then, I would read the entire file content using `file.read()`. I would split the content into words using `content.split()` and then use `len()` to count the number of words.

6. Question: You want to create a program that appends user-entered data to a file, with each entry on a new line. How would you do this?

Answer: I would open the file in append ('a') mode. Then, I would take user input using `input()`. I would write the input to the file using `file.write(input_data + '\n')`.

7. Question: How do you handle the potential `FileNotFoundError` when trying to open a file in Python?

Answer: I would use a `try-except` block. In the `try` block, I would attempt to open the file. In the `except FileNotFoundError` block, I would handle the error (e.g., print an error message or create the file).

8. Question: You have a CSV file that you want to read and process. How would you read the file and store the data in a list of lists?

Answer: I would use the `csv` module. I would open the file in read ('r') mode and create a `csv.reader` object. Then, I would iterate through the rows of the CSV file and append each row to a list.

9. Question: How do you ensure that a file is closed properly even if an exception occurs during file operations?

Answer: I would use the `with` statement. The `with` statement automatically closes the file, even if exceptions occur within the block.

10. Question: You need to create a file and write a list of numbers to it, with each number on a new line. How would you achieve this?

Answer: I would open the file in write ('w') mode. Then, I would iterate through the list of numbers. For each number, I would convert it to a string using `str()` and write it to the file using `file.write(str(number) + '\n')`.

CHAPTER 8: ERROR AND EXCEPTION HANDLING

In this chapter, we will explore how Python handles errors and exceptions, which is crucial for writing robust programs that can handle unexpected situations gracefully.

1. Understanding Errors in Python

a) Syntax Errors vs Runtime Errors

- **Syntax Errors:** Syntax errors occur when the Python code does not follow the proper syntax rules. These are typically detected by the Python interpreter when the program is being parsed (before it is executed). Syntax errors are often caused by missing or incorrect punctuation, incorrect indentation, or other formatting issues.

  Example:

  ```
  print("Hello World"  # Missing closing parenthesis
  ```

  Output:

  ```
  SyntaxError: unexpected EOF while parsing
  ```

  Explanation: The error occurs because there is a missing closing parenthesis for the `print` function. The interpreter cannot parse the code correctly without the proper syntax.

- **Runtime Errors:** Runtime errors occur during the execution of the program when Python encounters an operation it cannot perform. These errors occur after the program has passed the syntax check and are usually caused by logical mistakes, invalid operations, or unavailable resources.

  Example:

  ```
  x = 10 / 0  # Division by zero
  ```

  Output:

  ```
  ZeroDivisionError: division by zero
  ```

  Explanation: Here, a runtime error occurs because division by zero is mathematically undefined. The program stops executing when the error is encountered.

2. Exception Handling Basics

In Python, **exception handling** provides a way to gracefully handle runtime errors. Instead of abruptly stopping the program, exception handling allows you to respond to errors, ensuring the program can continue or terminate cleanly. Below, we explore the basics of exception handling and common scenarios.

---

a) try, except, finally Blocks

1. try Block

- The **try block** contains the code that might raise an exception (error).
- If an exception occurs, Python immediately stops executing the code in the try block and moves to the corresponding **except** block.

2. except Block

- The **except** block is where you handle specific exceptions.
- You can define multiple except blocks for different types of exceptions, or a single generic block to handle any error.

3. finally Block

- The **finally** block contains code that will always run, regardless of whether an exception was raised or not.
- This block is commonly used for cleanup tasks, such as closing files, releasing resources, or logging information.

Basic Syntax and Example
```
try:
    # Code that might raise an exception
    result = 10 / 0  # Risky code
except ZeroDivisionError:
    # Code to handle the exception
    print("Cannot divide by zero!")
finally:
    # Code that runs regardless of an exception
    print("This will always execute.")
```
Explanation

- **try Block**: Contains the risky code (10 / 0). Dividing by zero raises a ZeroDivisionError.
- **except Block**: Catches the ZeroDivisionError and handles it by printing a message.

- **`finally` Block**: Executes no matter what, ensuring necessary cleanup tasks are performed.

Output
```
Cannot divide by zero!
This will always execute.
```

b) Catching Multiple Exceptions

Python allows handling different types of exceptions using multiple **except** blocks. Each block is designed to catch a specific type of error. If none of the specified exceptions match, you can use a generic **Exception** block to catch unexpected errors.

Example
```
try:
    value = int(input("Enter a number: "))  # May raise ValueError
    result = 10 / value  # May raise ZeroDivisionError
except ZeroDivisionError:
    print("Cannot divide by zero!")
except ValueError:
    print("Invalid input! Please enter a valid number.")
except Exception as e:
    print(f"An unexpected error occurred: {e}")
finally:
    print("Execution completed.")
```
Explanation

1. **`try` Block**:
   - Accepts input from the user and tries to convert it to an integer.
   - Attempts division by the input value.
2. **`except` Blocks**:
   - **`ZeroDivisionError`**: Handles division by zero (e.g., when the user enters 0).
   - **`ValueError`**: Handles invalid numeric input (e.g., when the user enters a non-numeric value).
   - **Generic `Exception`**: Catches any other unexpected errors. The variable e holds the error message for debugging.
3. **`finally` Block**:
   - Executes cleanup tasks like logging or displaying a completion message, regardless of whether an exception occurred.

Example Outputs

1. **Case 1: ZeroDivisionError**

```
Enter a number: 0
Cannot divide by zero!
Execution completed.
```

2. Case 2: ValueError

```
Enter a number: hello
Invalid input! Please enter a valid number.
Execution completed.
```

3. Case 3: Generic Exception

```
Enter a number: -5
Execution completed.
```

Key Features of Exception Handling

1. **Flexibility:**
   o Allows programs to handle specific errors gracefully and avoid abrupt termination.
2. **Multiple Exception Blocks:**
   o Different types of errors can be handled separately for better clarity and control.
3. **Generic Exception Handling:**
   o Catch-all mechanism for unexpected errors to prevent program crashes.
4. **finally Block:**
   o Ensures critical cleanup code is executed regardless of errors.

Best Practices for Exception Handling

1. **Handle Specific Exceptions:**
   o Avoid using generic `Exception` unless necessary, as it may mask underlying issues.
2. **Log Errors:**
   o Use logging mechanisms to capture details of the exception for debugging and maintenance.
3. **Minimize Risky Code:**
   o Keep the **try block** small and isolate risky operations.
4. **Use `finally` Wisely:**
   o Ensure that resources like files or database connections are properly closed in the `finally` block.

Advanced Notes

- **else Block**:
  - Python also provides an **else** block, which executes only if no exceptions are raised in the try block.

```
try:
    result = 10 / 2
except ZeroDivisionError:
    print("Cannot divide by zero!")
else:
    print("No errors occurred. Result:", result)
finally:
    print("Execution completed.")
```

Output:

```
No errors occurred. Result: 5.0
Execution completed.
```

- **Raising Exceptions**:
  - You can explicitly raise exceptions using the **raise** keyword.

```
value = -1
if value < 0:
    raise ValueError("Negative value is not allowed!")
```

MCQ

1. What type of error is caused by incorrect syntax in Python?

A) Runtime Error
B) Syntax Error
C) Logical Error
D) Name Error

Answer: B) Syntax Error

---

2. Which of the following is a runtime error?

A) IndentationError
B) SyntaxError
C) ZeroDivisionError
D) ImportError

Answer: C) ZeroDivisionError

---

3. Which of the following is used to catch an exception in Python?

A) try
B) except
C) finally
D) All of the above

Answer: D) All of the above

---

4. What is the purpose of the `finally` block in Python?

A) To handle exceptions
B) To execute code no matter what
C) To raise exceptions
D) To catch errors

Answer: B) To execute code no matter what

---

5. Which block is executed only if no exception occurs in the `try` block?

A) try
B) except
C) finally
D) else

Answer: D) else

---

6. What happens if no exception occurs in the `try` block?

A) The `except` block is executed
B) The `finally` block is executed
C) The `else` block is executed
D) Both B and C

Answer: D) Both B and C

---

7. Which of the following is correct for handling multiple exceptions in Python?

A) Multiple `except` blocks
B) Only one `except` block
C) One `except` block with multiple exceptions separated by commas
D) Both A and C

Answer: D) Both A and C

---

8. Which of the following will not cause an exception in Python?

A) Opening a non-existent file
B) Dividing a number by zero
C) Trying to access an index out of range in a list
D) Assigning a value to a variable

Answer: D) Assigning a value to a variable

---

9. Which exception is raised when an integer is divided by zero?

A) ZeroDivisionError
B) IndexError
C) TypeError
D) ValueError

Answer: A) ZeroDivisionError

---

10. Which of the following is the correct syntax for handling an exception?

A) try: except:
B) try: except: finally:

C) try: finally: except:
D) except: try:

Answer: B) try: except: finally:

---

11. What will happen if an exception is not handled in a Python program?

A) The program will continue executing
B) The program will display an error message and stop execution
C) The program will restart
D) The program will ignore the error and continue

Answer: B) The program will display an error message and stop execution

---

12. What is raised when a variable is not defined in Python?

A) TypeError
B) NameError
C) ValueError
D) IndexError

Answer: B) NameError

---

13. How do you raise a custom exception in Python?

A) raise ExceptionType("message")
B) throw ExceptionType("message")
C) raise("message")
D) except ExceptionType("message")

Answer: A) raise ExceptionType("message")

---

14. What is the use of `else` block in error handling?

A) To define an exception
B) To execute code only if no exception occurs in the `try` block

C) To raise an exception

D) To catch exceptions

Answer: B) To execute code only if no exception occurs in the `try` block

---

15. What is the exception raised when a value cannot be converted to the required type?

A) ValueError

B) TypeError

C) KeyError

D) AttributeError

Answer: A) ValueError

---

16. Which of the following is the correct syntax for the `try` block in Python?

A) try: except:

B) try {} except {}

C) try{} catch{}

D) try: except:

Answer: A) try: except:

---

17. What happens if the `finally` block contains an error?

A) The exception is ignored

B) The `finally` block is skipped

C) The exception is raised

D) The program crashes

Answer: C) The exception is raised

---

18. Which exception is raised when there is a mismatch in data types?

A) TypeError
B) ValueError
C) KeyError
D) SyntaxError

Answer: A) TypeError

---

19. What is the outcome of the following code snippet?

```
try:
    x = int("hello")
except ValueError:
    print("Invalid value")
else:
    print("Valid value")
```

A) Valid value
B) Invalid value
C) It will cause a runtime error
D) It will print both "Invalid value" and "Valid value"

Answer: B) Invalid value

---

20. What is the correct way to handle a division by zero error in Python?

A) try: 1/0 except ZeroDivisionError: handle error
B) try: 1/0 except ValueError: handle error
C) try: 1/0 except IndexError: handle error
D) try: 1/0 except TypeError: handle error

Answer: A) try: 1/0 except ZeroDivisionError: handle error

---

21. Which of the following is a built-in exception in Python?

A) MyError
B) ZeroDivisionError
C) OutOfMemoryError
D) FileError

Answer: B) ZeroDivisionError

22. What is the purpose of using `finally` block?

A) To execute code after the `try` block no matter what
B) To define the exception
C) To handle exceptions
D) To exit from the function

Answer: A) To execute code after the `try` block no matter what

23. What is the result of the following code?

```
try:
    x = 10 / 0
except ZeroDivisionError as e:
    print(e)
finally:
    print("Executed Finally Block")
```

A) ZeroDivisionError
B) Executed Finally Block
C) ZeroDivisionError and Executed Finally Block
D) Nothing will be printed

Answer: C) ZeroDivisionError and Executed Finally Block

24. How can we define a custom exception in Python?

A) Define a class that inherits from `Exception`
B) Use the `raise` keyword
C) Use `try` and `except`
D) None of the above

Answer: A) Define a class that inherits from `Exception`

25. What happens if the `try` block raises an exception but there is no matching `except` block?

A) The program continues to execute
B) The program stops and an error message is displayed
C) The exception is automatically handled
D) It will call the `finally` block

Answer: B) The program stops and an error message is displayed

26. Which exception occurs when an item is accessed using a key that doesn't exist in a dictionary?

A) KeyError
B) IndexError
C) ValueError
D) NameError

Answer: A) KeyError

27. What does the following code do?

```
try:
    a = int(input("Enter a number: "))
    result = 10 / a
except ZeroDivisionError:
    print("Cannot divide by zero.")
except ValueError:
    print("Invalid input.")
finally:
    print("Execution completed.")
```

A) Handles only `ZeroDivisionError`
B) Handles only `ValueError`
C) Handles both `ZeroDivisionError` and `ValueError`
D) It will raise an exception if input is invalid

Answer: C) Handles both `ZeroDivisionError` and `ValueError`

28. What is the output of the following code?

```
try:
```

```
    num = int("hello")
except ValueError:
    print("Invalid input")
else:
    print("Valid input")
finally:
    print("Execution finished")
```

A) Invalid input
B) Valid input
C) Invalid input and Execution finished
D) Execution finished

Answer: C) Invalid input and Execution finished

29. Which of the following is used to handle errors and prevent program termination in Python?

A) Debugging
B) Exception handling
C) Logging
D) Assertions

Answer: B) Exception handling

30. What is the purpose of the `else` block in Python exception handling?

A) To execute code only if no exception occurs in the `try` block
B) To define custom exceptions
C) To handle exceptions
D) To terminate the program

Answer: A) To execute code only if no exception occurs in the `try` block

25 and answers covering Understanding Errors in Python and Exception Handling Basics:

Understanding Errors in Python

1. **Question:** What is the fundamental difference between a syntax error and a runtime error in Python? **Answer:** Syntax errors occur during parsing before

execution due to incorrect code structure, while runtime errors occur during execution when the program encounters an operation it can't perform.

2. **Question:** Provide an example of a common syntax error and explain how the Python interpreter detects it. **Answer:** Missing a colon in an `if` statement: `if x > 0 print("Positive")`. The interpreter detects it because it violates the expected syntax for `if` statements.

3. **Question:** Give an example of a runtime error and explain why it occurs during execution. **Answer:** Accessing an index out of range in a list: `my_list = [1, 2, 3]; print(my_list[5])`. It occurs because the index 5 does not exist in the list.

4. **Question:** Why are syntax errors generally easier to fix than runtime errors? **Answer:** Syntax errors are detected before execution and often provide clear error messages, while runtime errors require debugging to trace the execution flow and identify the issue.

5. **Question:** How does the Python interpreter handle a syntax error when it encounters one? **Answer:** The interpreter stops parsing and displays a `SyntaxError` message, indicating the location and type of the error.

Exception Handling Basics

6. **Question:** Explain the purpose of the `try-except` block in Python. **Answer:** The `try-except` block allows you to handle runtime errors (exceptions) gracefully, preventing the program from crashing.

7. **Question:** Describe the role of the `try` block in exception handling. **Answer:** The `try` block contains the code that might raise an exception.

8. **Question:** What is the purpose of the `except` block, and how does it relate to the `try` block? **Answer:** The `except` block handles specific exceptions that might occur in the `try` block.

9. **Question:** Explain the function of the `finally` block in exception handling. **Answer:** The `finally` block contains code that always executes, whether an exception occurred or not. It's used for cleanup tasks.

10. **Question:** Provide an example of using a `try-except-finally` block to handle a `ZeroDivisionError`. **Answer:**

Python

```
try:
    result = 10 / 0
except ZeroDivisionError:
    print("Cannot divide by zero.")
finally:
    print("This always executes.")
```

11. **Question:** How do you catch multiple exceptions in a single `try-except` block? **Answer:** Use multiple `except` blocks, each specifying a different exception type.

12. **Question:** Explain the purpose of catching a generic `Exception` in Python. **Answer:** Catching a generic `Exception` handles any unexpected errors that don't match specific `except` blocks.

13. **Question:** Give an example of catching a `ValueError` when converting user input to an integer. **Answer:**

```
try:
    value = int(input("Enter a number: "))
except ValueError:
    print("Invalid input.")
```

14. **Question:** How does the `else` block in a `try-except` statement function? **Answer:** The `else` block executes only if no exceptions are raised in the `try` block.
15. **Question:** Explain how to explicitly raise an exception using the `raise` keyword. **Answer:** Use `raise ExceptionType("message")` to raise a specific exception with an optional message.
16. **Question:** Why is it important to handle specific exceptions rather than relying solely on a generic `Exception`? **Answer:** Handling specific exceptions allows for targeted error handling and avoids masking underlying issues.
17. **Question:** Describe a scenario where you would use the `finally` block for cleanup tasks. **Answer:** Closing a file or releasing a network resource, ensuring they are always closed regardless of exceptions.
18. **Question:** How can logging be used in exception handling to improve debugging? **Answer:** Logging captures details of exceptions, including error messages and stack traces, for later analysis.
19. **Question:** What are best practices for minimizing the code within a `try` block? **Answer:** Keep the `try` block small and isolate only the code that might raise an exception.
20. **Question:** Explain how to use the `as` keyword to store an exception instance in a variable. **Answer:** `except Exception as e:` stores the exception instance in the variable `e`, allowing access to its attributes.
21. **Question:** How does Python's exception handling promote code robustness? **Answer:** It allows programs to gracefully handle errors, preventing abrupt termination and ensuring continued operation.
22. **Question:** When would you use a `try-except` block within a loop? **Answer:** When you need to handle exceptions that might occur during each iteration of the loop.
23. **Question:** How can you create a custom exception in Python? **Answer:** Define a new class that inherits from the `Exception` class.
24. **Question:** Explain how the stack trace helps in debugging runtime errors. **Answer:** The stack trace shows the sequence of function calls leading to the error, helping to pinpoint the source of the problem.
25. **Question:** Why is it important to provide informative error messages when raising or handling exceptions? **Answer:** Informative error messages help developers understand the cause of the error and troubleshoot effectively.

Practical Examples

a) Handle Division by Zero Error

Division by zero is a common runtime error. Using exception handling, we can catch this error and display a meaningful message instead of allowing the program to crash.

Example:

```
def divide(a, b):
    try:
        result = a / b
    except ZeroDivisionError:
        print("Error: Division by zero is not allowed.")
    else:
        print(f"The result is: {result}")
    finally:
        print("Execution completed.")

# Test with valid and invalid inputs
divide(10, 2)   # Valid input
divide(10, 0)   # Division by zero
```

Output:

```
The result is: 5.0
Execution completed.
Error: Division by zero is not allowed.
Execution completed.
```

Explanation:

- The `divide` function attempts to divide `a` by `b`.
- If `b` is `0`, the `ZeroDivisionError` is caught by the `except` block.
- The `else` block runs if no exception occurs.
- The `finally` block runs after both `try` and `except` blocks, ensuring that the program finishes cleanly.

---

b) Check for Invalid Input

Sometimes, input validation is required to ensure that the user provides the correct type of data. If the input is invalid, we can handle it gracefully using exception handling.

Example:

```
def get_positive_integer():
    try:
        number = int(input("Enter a positive integer: "))
        if number <= 0:
```

```
        raise ValueError("The number must be positive.")
    except ValueError as e:
        print(f"Invalid input: {e}")
    else:
        print(f"You entered: {number}")
    finally:
        print("Input process completed.")

# Test with valid and invalid inputs
get_positive_integer()  # Invalid input: non-integer or negative number
```

Output (for invalid input):

```
Enter a positive integer: -5
Invalid input: The number must be positive.
Input process completed.
```

Explanation:

- The `try` block attempts to convert the input to an integer.
- If the input is not an integer, a `ValueError` will be raised and caught by the `except` block.
- The `else` block executes if no error occurs, and the number is positive.
- The `finally` block ensures that the input process is always completed, regardless of the outcome.

---

4. Custom Exceptions

You can also define your own exceptions by subclassing the built-in `Exception` class. This allows you to create more meaningful error messages specific to your application.

Example:

```
class NegativeNumberError(Exception):
    def __init__(self, message):
        self.message = message
        super().__init__(self.message)

def check_number(num):
    if num < 0:
        raise NegativeNumberError("Negative numbers are not allowed.")
    else:
        print(f"The number {num} is valid.")

try:
    check_number(-5)
except NegativeNumberError as e:
    print(e)
```

Output:

```
Negative numbers are not allowed.
```

Explanation:

- A custom exception `NegativeNumberError` is created by subclassing `Exception`.
- The function `check_number` raises this exception if the input is negative.
- The `try` block catches and prints the custom error message.

1. Handling File Not Found Error

Scenario: Trying to open a file that does not exist.

```
try:
    with open("nonexistent_file.txt", "r") as file:
        content = file.read()
except FileNotFoundError:
    print("Error: The file was not found.")
finally:
    print("Execution completed.")
```

Output:

```
Error: The file was not found.
Execution completed.
```

Explanation:

- The program attempts to open a file that does not exist. Since the file is missing, it raises a `FileNotFoundError`, which is caught by the `except` block.

2. Handling Index Out of Range Error

Scenario: Accessing an invalid index in a list.

```
my_list = [1, 2, 3]

try:
    print(my_list[5])  # Invalid index
except IndexError:
    print("Error: List index out of range.")
finally:
    print("Execution completed.")
```

Output:

```
Error: List index out of range.
Execution completed.
```

Explanation:

- The program tries to access an index that does not exist in the list. The `IndexError` is caught and handled by the `except` block.

3. Handling Value Error in User Input

Scenario: Invalid input that cannot be converted to an integer.

```
try:
    num = int(input("Enter a number: "))
except ValueError:
    print("Error: Invalid input. Please enter an integer.")
finally:
    print("Input process completed.")
```

Output (for invalid input like 'abc'):

```
Enter a number: abc
Error: Invalid input. Please enter an integer.
Input process completed.
```

Explanation:

- The `ValueError` is raised if the user inputs a non-integer value. The `except` block catches it and displays an error message.

4. Handling Division by Zero with Custom Error Message

Scenario: Handling division by zero with a custom error message.

```
try:
    a = int(input("Enter numerator: "))
    b = int(input("Enter denominator: "))
    result = a / b
except ZeroDivisionError:
    print("Error: Cannot divide by zero.")
except ValueError:
    print("Error: Please enter valid integers.")
else:
    print(f"Result: {result}")
```

```
finally:
    print("Execution completed.")
```

Output (for denominator as zero):

```
Enter numerator: 10
Enter denominator: 0
Error: Cannot divide by zero.
Execution completed.
```

Explanation:

- This program checks for both `ZeroDivisionError` and `ValueError` exceptions and handles them accordingly.

---

5. Handling Multiple Exceptions

Scenario: Handling multiple exceptions like `ZeroDivisionError` and `ValueError`.

```
try:
    a = int(input("Enter numerator: "))
    b = int(input("Enter denominator: "))
    result = a / b
except ZeroDivisionError:
    print("Error: Cannot divide by zero.")
except ValueError:
    print("Error: Invalid input. Please enter integers.")
except Exception as e:
    print(f"Unexpected error: {e}")
else:
    print(f"Result: {result}")
finally:
    print("Execution completed.")
```

Output (for invalid input):

```
Enter numerator: 10
Enter denominator: abc
Error: Invalid input. Please enter integers.
Execution completed.
```

Explanation:

- The program handles multiple errors with different `except` blocks and displays relevant messages based on the exception type.

---

6. Handling Negative Value Error

Scenario: Ensuring a positive number is entered by the user.

```
def check_positive(num):
    if num < 0:
        raise ValueError("Number must be positive.")
    else:
        print(f"Valid number: {num}")

try:
    num = int(input("Enter a positive number: "))
    check_positive(num)
except ValueError as e:
    print(f"Error: {e}")
finally:
    print("Execution completed.")
```

Output (for negative input):

```
Enter a positive number: -5
Error: Number must be positive.
Execution completed.
```

Explanation:

- A `ValueError` is raised manually when a negative number is entered, and it's caught in the `except` block.

---

7. Handling KeyError in Dictionary Access

Scenario: Attempting to access a key that doesn't exist in a dictionary.

```
my_dict = {"name": "Alice", "age": 30}

try:
    print(my_dict["address"])  # Key does not exist
except KeyError:
    print("Error: Key not found in the dictionary.")
finally:
    print("Execution completed.")
```

Output:

```
Error: Key not found in the dictionary.
Execution completed.
```

Explanation:

- The program attempts to access a key that doesn't exist in the dictionary, resulting in a `KeyError` which is caught and handled by the `except` block.

---

8. Handling TypeError in Addition

Scenario: Performing an operation with incompatible data types.

```
try:
    result = "Hello" + 5  # Trying to add string and integer
except TypeError:
    print("Error: Cannot concatenate string and integer.")
finally:
    print("Execution completed.")
```

Output:

```
Error: Cannot concatenate string and integer.
Execution completed.
```

Explanation:

- The program tries to add a string and an integer, causing a `TypeError`. The `except` block handles the error by printing a message.

---

9. Handling Multiple Exceptions with Specific Order

Scenario: Catching `IndexError`, `ValueError`, and `TypeError`.

```
try:
    my_list = [1, 2, 3]
    print(my_list[5])  # IndexError
    num = int(input("Enter a number: "))
except IndexError:
    print("Error: List index out of range.")
except ValueError:
    print("Error: Invalid value entered.")
except TypeError:
    print("Error: Type mismatch.")
finally:
    print("Execution completed.")
```

Output:

```
Error: List index out of range.
Execution completed.
```

Explanation:

- The `IndexError` is caught first because the invalid index is accessed before the input for the number is taken.

---

10. Handling AttributeError

Scenario: Trying to access a non-existent method or attribute of an object.

```python
class MyClass:
    def greet(self):
        print("Hello, world!")

obj = MyClass()

try:
    obj.greeting()  # Method does not exist
except AttributeError:
    print("Error: Method not found.")
finally:
    print("Execution completed.")
```

Output:

```
Error: Method not found.
Execution completed.
```

Explanation:

- The program attempts to call a non-existent method `greeting()` on the object `obj`. This causes an `AttributeError`, which is caught and handled in the `except` block.

CHAPTER 9: PYTHON AND MINI PROJECTS

In this chapter, we will explore some beginner-level project ideas that will help you understand how to apply basic Python concepts. These projects are designed to reinforce your skills in handling data, using conditions, loops, lists, and files, as well as structuring code effectively.

---

1. Simple Calculator

Objective:

Create a basic calculator that can perform simple arithmetic operations such as addition, subtraction, multiplication, and division.

Concepts Covered:

- Functions
- Conditional statements (if-else)
- User input
- Error handling (e.g., division by zero)

Code Example:
```python
def add(x, y):
    return x + y

def subtract(x, y):
    return x - y

def multiply(x, y):
    return x * y

def divide(x, y):
    if y == 0:
        return "Error! Division by zero."
    return x / y

# Main program
print("Select operation:")
print("1. Add")
print("2. Subtract")
print("3. Multiply")
print("4. Divide")

choice = input("Enter choice(1/2/3/4): ")

num1 = float(input("Enter first number: "))
num2 = float(input("Enter second number: "))

if choice == '1':
```

```
    print(f"{num1} + {num2} = {add(num1, num2)}")
elif choice == '2':
    print(f"{num1} - {num2} = {subtract(num1, num2)}")
elif choice == '3':
    print(f"{num1} * {num2} = {multiply(num1, num2)}")
elif choice == '4':
    print(f"{num1} / {num2} = {divide(num1, num2)}")
else:
    print("Invalid input")
```

Explanation:

- The program defines four functions for each arithmetic operation: `add()`, `subtract()`, `multiply()`, and `divide()`.
- It then takes user input for the operation and the numbers to perform the calculation.
- Error handling is included for division by zero.

---

2. Grade Checker (Using if-else Statements)

Objective:

Create a grade checker program that takes the user's marks and assigns a grade based on the provided scale.

Concepts Covered:

- Conditional statements (if-else)
- User input

Code Example:
```
def grade_checker(marks):
    if marks >= 90:
        return "A+"
    elif marks >= 80:
        return "A"
    elif marks >= 70:
        return "B"
    elif marks >= 60:
        return "C"
    elif marks >= 50:
        return "D"
    else:
        return "F"

marks = float(input("Enter your marks: "))
grade = grade_checker(marks)
print(f"Your grade is: {grade}")
```

Explanation:

- The function `grade_checker()` uses multiple `if-else` conditions to determine the grade based on the marks entered by the user.
- The program checks whether the marks fall within certain ranges and assigns a corresponding grade.

3. Number Guessing Game (Using Loops and Conditions)

Objective:

Create a game where the user has to guess a randomly generated number between 1 and 100.

Concepts Covered:

- Loops (while)
- Random number generation
- Conditional statements (if-else)

Code Example:
```
import random

def number_guessing_game():
    number_to_guess = random.randint(1, 100)
    attempts = 0
    while True:
        guess = int(input("Guess a number between 1 and 100: "))
        attempts += 1

        if guess < number_to_guess:
            print("Too low! Try again.")
        elif guess > number_to_guess:
            print("Too high! Try again.")
        else:
            print(f"Congratulations! You guessed the number in
{attempts} attempts.")
            break

number_guessing_game()
```
Explanation:

- The `random.randint()` function generates a random number between 1 and 100.
- A `while` loop is used to allow the user to keep guessing until they get the correct number.
- If the guess is too low or too high, the program provides feedback, otherwise, it congratulates the user when they guess correctly.

4. Basic Student Management System (Using Lists and Files)

Objective:

Create a student management system where you can add student details (name, age, grade) and save them to a file. The system should also allow you to retrieve and display the saved data.

Concepts Covered:

- Lists
- File handling (reading and writing to a file)
- User input
- Functions

Code Example:

```
import os

def add_student(students):
    name = input("Enter student name: ")
    age = input("Enter student age: ")
    grade = input("Enter student grade: ")
    student = {'name': name, 'age': age, 'grade': grade}
    students.append(student)
    save_to_file(students)

def save_to_file(students):
    with open("students.txt", "w") as file:
        for student in students:

file.write(f"{student['name']},{student['age']},{student['grade']}\n")

def load_from_file():
    students = []
    if os.path.exists("students.txt"):
        with open("students.txt", "r") as file:
            for line in file:
                name, age, grade = line.strip().split(",")
                students.append({'name': name, 'age': age, 'grade':
grade})
    return students

def display_students(students):
    if students:
        print("Student List:")
        for student in students:
            print(f"Name: {student['name']}, Age: {student['age']},
Grade: {student['grade']}")
    else:
        print("No students found.")

def student_management_system():
    students = load_from_file()
```

```
while True:
        print("\n1. Add Student")
        print("2. Display Students")
        print("3. Exit")

        choice = input("Enter your choice: ")

        if choice == '1':
            add_student(students)
        elif choice == '2':
            display_students(students)
        elif choice == '3':
            break
        else:
            print("Invalid choice. Please try again.")

student_management_system()
```

Explanation:

- This program uses a list of dictionaries to store student details.
- The `add_student()` function collects student information and appends it to the list.
- The `save_to_file()` function writes the student details to a file, while `load_from_file()` reads the file and loads the student details when the program starts.
- The system provides options to add students, display the list of students, or exit the program.

Conclusion:

These mini-projects are designed to give beginners a hands-on understanding of Python's basic concepts. By working through these examples, you will get comfortable with:

- Handling user input and providing output
- Working with loops, conditionals, and functions
- Managing data using lists and files
- Writing and reading files to store persistent data

As you get more comfortable with these basic projects, you can expand them by adding more features, error handling, or even graphical interfaces.

172